P9-CSW-261

Labor, Solidarity and
the Common Good

Labor, Solidarity and the Common Good

Essays on the Ethical
Foundations of Management

Edited by

S.A. Cortright

Carolina Academic Press
Durham, North Carolina

Copyright © 2001
S.A. Cortright
All Rights Reserved

Library of Congress Cataloging-in-Publication

Labor, solidarity and the common good / edited by S.A. Cortright.
    p. cm.
    Includes bibliographic references and indexes.
    ISBN 0-89089-718-2
    1. Sociology, Christian (Catholic). 2. Catholic Church—
Doctrines. 3. Christian ethics—Catholic authors. I. Cortright,
S.A. (Steven A.), 1953–

BX1753.L15 2000
261.8'5—dc21   00-036106

Publication of this volume is due in part to
The Trust Funds, Inc., San Francisco, California.

Carolina Academic Press
700 Kent Street
Durham, North Carolina 27701
Telephone (919) 489-7486
Facsimile (919) 493-5668
E-mail: cap@cap-press.com
www.cap-press.com

Printed in the United States of America.

Contents

Preface

The papers collected in this volume grew out of the inaugural conference of the John F. Henning Institute, *Labor, Solidarity and the Common Good*, on the campus of Saint Mary's College of California, January 18, 1997. Special thanks is owing to the Y. Charles and Helen Soda Foundation, whose generous support made the conference possible, and to The Trust Funds, Inc. of San Francisco, through whose generous support this volume was assembled and edited.

Founded on the conviction that philosophical inquiry and scholarship are essential to the promotion of the common good, the Henning Institute seeks to foster exploration of Catholic social thought — its philosophical and theological bases, and its implications for public policy — both as developed in the Papal Encyclicals from *Rerum novarum* forward, and in relation to other moral traditions dedicated to the common good. The Institute's motto, *"...for the Dignity of Work and the Worker,"* underscores its dedication to scholarship which attends to the transcendent dignity of the human person, to the dignity of human work and the worker, and to the centrality of human labor in the realization of the common good.

The Institute's orientation and efforts are inspired by the life and work of its namesake, John F. Henning. Throughout a career which has taken him into the counsels of government and diplomacy — as United States Under Secretary of Labor and Ambassador to New Zealand — and has placed him, during twenty-six years as Executive Secretary-Treasurer of the California Labor Federation, AFL-CIO, at the forefront of the American labor movement, Mr. Henning has passionately pursued the common good in light of the principles of Catholic social thought. A forceful advocate in the world of public affairs, never prone to confuse a position's popularity with its rightness, neither has he forgotten that civil discourse at the level of first principles can transcend political and ideological differences, to the benefit of all. Fittingly, then, Mr. Henning describes Leo XIII's *Rerum novarum* as his "first book"; so, too, is *Rerum novarum* the first book of the Institute which bears his name, and is proud to celebrate and to advance his legacy.

Because the John F. Henning Institute seeks particularly to foster the development of younger scholars, there is reason to take special satisfaction in this volume of proceedings. The contributors and respondents are accomplished scholars; from most, we may expect to hear for decades hence. If, as James Murphy proposes in these pages, recent developments in Catholic social thought are "a sign of hope for our times," we may take increased hope from the likelihood that the contributors to *Labor, Solidarity and the Common Good* will, for many years to come, pioneer further stages in the road that leads from *Rerum novarum*.

Saint Mary's College of California
February 2000

Labor, Solidarity and the Common Good

Introduction

Human Work, Hinge of the Social Question

S. A. Cortright*
Ernest S. Pierucci*

To flourish as a person, to live free and never as another's instrument, to take meaningful part in the human community: these aspirations engage at once the untutored desire of every human being and the most profound philosophical and theological reflection. In no connection is their theoretical grounding or their practical feasibility more deeply challenged than in pursuit of the question, What is the nature of work? Indeed, according to the classical opposition of liberal to servile (or, immanent to transitive) activity, being given over to work—to servile, transitive activity—was the very definition of the slave, while relief from the need to work was the condition of one's growth into full humanity. Jacques Maritain surveyed the historical sweep of the opposition between what belongs to work and what belongs to human fulfillment:

> The concept of man, as to practical and social application, was itself, to tell the truth, unconsciously restricted. The only people in whom the concept of man had succeeded in displaying its full implications were in antiquity those men who enjoyed the condition of free men, in contrast to slaves; later on, and over a long period of time, they were admittedly, as a matter of fact, those men who enjoyed possibilities for leisure, and guiding responsibilities with respect to the mass—say, noblemen or gentlemen, or members of the third estate, or, after the Industrial Revolution, members of the upper bourgeoisie, in contrast to tradesmen and manual workers. Humanity, for all practical purposes, was represented in them. *Humanum paucis vivit genus*. The human race lives in a few, and for a few: this motto was a matter of consent from Ancient Greece and

Aristotle on to the advent of a better realization of the Christian message's temporal implications.[1]

Catholic social thought can be summarized as the explication of the Christian message's temporal implications. Its project: to set forth, philosophically and theologically, the whole difference the Incarnation has wrought for fundamental human aspirations. The project, especially as it concerns the question of human work, has grown the reverse of simpler; owing to the rise and waning of modernity, it has grown more urgent as well.

As modernity subsides into post-modernity, the moral landscape offers those who work few indications in what, ultimately, the meaning of their labor consists, and fewer clues how to claim that meaning. At the same time, work, always the usual human lot, has emerged also as the *common* human focus. The leisure class are a remnant, understood not as the bearers of humanity's essence, but as the moral equivalent of lottery winners—selected by chance for a perpetual vacation.

Meanwhile, those who still subscribe to the classical notion (identified above all with Aristotle), *viz.*, that work simply means a perfecting of the artifact at the expense of its maker, can offer, for the edification of the many consigned ineluctably to essentially "servile" pursuits, the consoling vision of a few engaged in "liberal work." Thus, as recently as 1988, Mortimer Adler reasserted the traditional view that work must remain largely a realm of purely transitive activity, servile because it subordinates the human subject to a universe of objects and objectives. Notwithstanding a few privileged occupations—physician, lawyer, professor or research scientist—the need to work amounts, at best, to an unappealable sentence to a radically divided life. Thus:

> The aristocratic error is simply the error of dividing men into free men and slaves or workers, into a leisure class and a working class, instead of dividing the time of each human life into working time and leisure time.[2]

On this account, while he is working the hospital orderly's activity is instrumentalized to the (relative) human perfection of the surgeon's. Be-

---

1. Jacques Maritain, "Education and the Humanities," in Donald and Idella Gallagher, eds., *The Education of Man* (New York: Doubleday, 1962), p. 87.

2. Mortimer Adler, "Labor, Leisure and Liberal Education," in Geraldine Van Doren, ed., *Reforming Education: The Opening of the American Mind* (New York: Macmillan Publishing, 1988), p. 106.

cause, that is, the surgeon knows, and acts for, the end-in-view, the orderly—no less than the scalpel—is the surgeon's instrument: while "on the job," he is "good" only "for" his use, only as an embodied function, so to speak. But the eight-hour day permits him another life: "off the job" he may be a devotee of the opera, an amateur historian... or a serious student of surgical technique; meanwhile, the democratic regime allows for his participation in the government of his community as well. Nevertheless, Adler's account consigns our orderly, *as a working person*, to a status scarcely distinguishable in principle from that of a Greek slave.

Modern and post-modern thought pose a different—perhaps, a greater—challenge to the project of Catholic social thought than is posed by the ambivalent legacy of classical, pagan antiquity. They deny that there is, on the natural level, a human end or *telos* in terms of which to articulate a notion of specifically human fulfillment, let alone the notion of common human ends, that is, of the common good.

Thus, the rise of modernity saw contract replace social status as the animating force of social relations, opening new realms of human development. This advance came, however, at a price. If the pre-modern error had been to divide persons into free and slave, the error of modernity was to conceive a strange equality: persons are essentially atoms of will, justly related (and relatable) only through just—*because* voluntary—contracts. The result is an economy embedded in a moral landscape that resists any appeal to a good common to all by virtue of their common humanity. William James Booth describes the impact of modernity on the economy:

> The mode of producing and distributing the means for human sustenance embodied in the market is expressive not of a human propensity to truck, trade and barter or of the desire to acquire ever more things, but rather of a moral redrawing of the community and of the place of the economy within it. What that transition yields is a new form of moral embeddedness for the economy. The attributes claimed for it are familiar: an economy whose actors are considered equals and a system indifferent to their noneconomic attributes; a contractarian, voluntaristic institutional context for exchanges; and the view that the public authority should not decide among the preferences—that one is entitled to live one's life "from the inside," selecting and ordering one's preferences according to the good as one

understands it and seeking to engage the voluntary cooperation of others in one's pursuit of them.[3]

Within modernity's moral landscape, work becomes a privately held commodity to be exchanged on the terms of voluntary contract. Likewise, property's private aspect is emphasized to the virtual exclusion of its social dimension. The social character of human life is understood as a construct erected out of voluntary agreements, and thus as the epiphenomenon of the pursuit of competing private interests. Put equivalently, human society is understood not as the achievement of practical understanding, but as the expression of will; and society is compacted through a calculated contraposition of inherently clashing wills, preferences, appetites. These developments cannot be dismissed simply as outgrowths of iron economic necessity or wayward human desire; rather, they express modernity's notion of the moral high-ground.

Under the modern regime, the worker is to be freed from service as the instrument of another's human fulfillment through the wholesale abandonment of the very notion of specifically human fulfillment in favor of the notion of individual preference. To argue on the basis of a teleological understanding of the person is to announce one's rejection of the essential modern achievement. Still, one may ask: where does modernity leave the worker, if not as the instrument of overweening preferences (some of which, with luck, might coincide with the worker's own)?

On the prevailing modern account, moreover, work cannot be explicated as an immanent act, for modern and post-modern thought recognize no authentically immanent human acts. With respect to work, the gravamen is, again, the atomistic, contractarian understanding of the person, which reduces work, without residue, to a commodity exchangeable under contract law, *i.e.*, at will. Doubtless, some features of the employment relationship correspond to this view, but the view betrays its obtuseness by its neglect of the fact that material compensation can never adequately reflect the value of any immanent human act. Modernity's insistence on the total commodification of human labor is the obverse of modernity's failure to recognize labor's immanent, subjective dimension.

If, then, Catholic social thought has learned from the ancient world an abiding concern for what is common, or specifically human, which sets it against the fundamental assumptions of modernity, it has also

---

3. William James Booth, "On the Idea of the Moral Economy," *American Political Science Review* Vol. 88, No. 3 (September 1994), p. 661.

learned from the figure of God Incarnate, carpenter and manual worker, that "...the value of human work is not primarily the kind of work being done but the fact that the one who is doing it is a person," and that "...*the primary basis of the value of work is man himself*, who is its subject."[4] Again, if Catholic social thought has thus learned to approach all work both as a transitive activity and as an immanent activity tending to the perfection of its human subject, it also finds in the subjective dimension of work the bases for an account of common—that is, social—specifically human—that is, determinate and compelling— ends or goods. Against the legacy of antiquity, then, Catholic social thought opposes an egalitarian valuation of labor; against the suppositions of modernity, it supposes a community of persons linked together by their participation in certain goods, including economic goods: that is to say, it proposes that human beings flourish only in and through common, shareable, goods.

When John Paul II writes, "...human labor is *as a hinge*, probably the principal hinge, for the whole social question," adding "....[I]f the solution [of the social question]...must be sought in consideration of how 'human life may be rendered more human,' then in truth the hinge, namely human work, acquires fundamental and decisive importance,"[5] we must take him in the vein of exact, sober description. For, the modern age has made work, has made laborious individual achievement, the cynosure of human life;[6] as the age wanes, where and to what it shall turn may itself turn on the question, What else shall be made of work? It will not come amiss here, therefore, to examine how, on the bases (1) of human labor's dual, immanent and transitive, character and its subjective value and (2) of its role in the promotion of common goods or ends, Catholic social thought may approach the looming question of human work.

---

4. John Paul II, *On Human Work (Laborem exercens)*, trans. Vatican Polyglot Press (Boston: St. Paul Editions, 1981), II. n. 6., pp. 15-16 (emphasis in original).

5. *Acta Ioannis Pauli PP. II, Litterae Encyclicae, "Laborem Exercens...," **Acta Apostolicae Sedis LXXII**, 5 Novembris, 1981* (Città del Vaticano: Libreria Editrice Vaticana), n. 3, p. 584: "...*laborem humanum esse **veluti cardinem**, probabiliter primarium, totius quaestiones socialis.... [S]i solutio...est quaerenda eo consilio ut vita humana humanior reddatur, tunc reapse ille cardo, id est labor humanus, momentum primarium obtinet ac decretorium.*" Cp. John Paul II, *op. cit.*, p. 10: "...human work is *a key*, probably *the essential key*, to the whole social question..."

6. Cf., *e.g.*, Josef Pieper, *Leisure, The Basis of Culture*, trans. Alexander Dru (New York: Pantheon Books, 1952), pp. 25-47, 61-71.

I

To John Paul II's *Laborem exercens* is owing a renewed attention to the human person as the subject of work which has, in its turn, revived interest in such allied, traditional Catholic social teachings as the just wage, the universal destination of goods, the principle of subsidiarity, and the moral foundations of the political economy. In *Laborem exercens*, as in *Sollicitudo rei socialis, Centesimus annus* and, indeed, throughout the range of documents produced in a pontificate remarkable for sustained attention to social questions, John Paul II is everywhere at pains to display his arguments as reflections—albeit, duly attentive to changed times and circumstances—on, and *of*, the principles laid down by his predecessors. On balance, the principles in question are Thomistic in provenance and intention; and, in *Laborem exercens*, John Paul II defers to both provenance and intention on such fundamentals as the nature of property and the right of its possession and use, citing relevant Questions of the *Summa Theologiae* and the explicitly Thomistic language of *Quadragesimo anno* to effect.[7] In connection with the nature of work, he borrows the concept of a *bonum arduum*—an arduous (human) good—from St. Thomas, and characterizes the virtues associated with work in classically Thomistic fashion[8] ... but all this to the end of supporting the decidedly extra-Thomistic propositions: (1) that work is an intrinsic human good, perfective as such of the agent; (2) that it depends upon the development of industriousness as a moral virtue.[9]

The latter juncture points up the fact that the Pope's revivifying effect on Catholic social thought owes something to the freedom with which he treats a largely Thomistic tradition; there is a modern cast to his thought, which (though hardly comforting to defenders of the modern regime) figures prominently in the centrally important reflections on work. Thus, the first task to confront anyone aiming at a just appreciation of contemporary Catholic social thought on work is to assess John Paul II's contribution to—and, perhaps, against—the tradition. James Bernard Murphy ably undertakes that task in the present volume's first essay, "The Quest for a Balanced Appraisal of Work in Catholic Social Thought."

---

7. Cf. John Paul II, *On Human Work (Laborem exercens)*, n. 14.

8. Cf. *ibid.*, n. 9.

9. See James Bernard Murphy, "The Quest for a Balanced Appraisal of Work in Catholic Social Thought," pp. 34-35, below.

Professor Murphy's learned and lucid essay revisits the sustained, philosophical responses to a familiar spectrum of conflicting intuitions on the value of work: work is the human genuflection to need, a necessary evil or (at best) the neutral instrument for the promotion of intrinsic human goods; work is the locus of human achievement and satisfactions, and so bids to be recognized as the highest human good; work is a unique source of personal fulfillment alongside other, intrinsic and incommensurable human goods, as friendship, worship, play....

Noting that traditional Catholic social thought is especially indebted to the Aristotelian-Thomistic view of work as an exclusively transitive activity, and thus an exclusively instrumental good, Professor Murphy traces the debt through successive documents of official Catholic teaching from *Rerum novarum* to *Laborem exercens*, arguing that the latter breaks explicitly and philosophically with the core tradition on work. In a concluding, telling critique of John Paul II's philosophy and theology of work, Professor Murphy makes a case for treating *Laborem exercens* as an over-correction: unbalanced in itself, but finally salutary in its influence over Catholic thought on work. Patrick Downey's response, "*Homo Reflectens*," offers a trenchant critique of the concept of "balanced appraisal" which informs Professor Murphy's argument.

II

Contracts are the ubiquitous vehicle of work-relationships and, perhaps, the signal institution of the modern age. *Rerum novarum* brings the wage contract in particular under severe scrutiny, but for reasons which implicate the modern notion of contract in general. Leo XIII insists that the parties' consent alone is insufficient to establish the justice of their contract; that in addition, objective criteria of equity, in the form of natural principles of justice—commutative and distributive—must be met.[10] In the special case of the wage contract, elements of distributive justice which ground the just wage theory predominate,[11] but Leo XIII's general position can be characterized as a firm rejection of the proposition that contracts simply consist in the consenting wills of the parties.[12]

---

10. Cf. Leo XIII, *On the Condition of the Working Classes (Rerum novarum)* (Boston: St. Paul Editions, 1978?), *e.g.*, n. 57: "...a man cannot even by his own free choice allow himself to be treated in a way inconsistent with his nature..."; cf. also *ibid.*, n. 30.

11. Cf. *ibid.*, ns. 61-63.

12. Cf., *e.g.*, *ibid.*, n. 60: "...no one has the right to demand of, or to make an agree-

Leo XIII calls particular attention to disparities in wealth, power and status between parties, not merely as these might constitute impediments to free consent, but as factors which may serve to manoeuvre one party into agreement on inequitable burdens or secure to a party inequitable advantages (in the case of contracted working conditions, *e.g.*, Leo XIII looks to union organization the means by which workers may come to a contract-negotiation on terms of relative parity with employers).[13] This concern is echoed and developed by Pius XI and, latterly, by John Paul II.[14] The tradition of official Catholic social teaching is, then, one in its rejection of any "will theory" of contract, just as the *philosophical* tendency of modernity is in favor of some, suitably elaborated, version of a "will theory," finding in it the mirror of the parties' personal autonomy.

In his essay, "Labor and Commutative Justice," James Gordley takes aim at an egregious fact: American courts, which do not explicitly recognize an equity doctrine of contract, nevertheless have, over the past century, built up *ad hoc* an enormous body of case law which might have been authored under Leo XIII's inspiration. The courts do not lack, Professor Gordley argues, a fine sense of what justice demands; they lack a coherent, consistent theory of contract which would serve to explain and harmonize their actual, largely salutary decisions.

In pursuit of the requisite doctrine, Professor Gordley returns us to the era of Upton Sinclair's *The Jungle*, when the courts routinely handed down rulings consistent with a thoroughgoing "will theory" of contract, but palpably inconsistent with rudimentary intuitions of the just. Drawing on the plight of Sinclair's hapless immigrant meatpackers, he shows how the courts, theoretically hamstrung, elaborated a groundwork of decisions which set them on a course of handing down intuitively equitable decisions, but justified on "creative" or otherwise dubious grounds. Having identified therewith a budget of justificatory problems in contract law, Professor Gordley demonstrates how these consistently yield, with virtually deductive ease, to the pre-modern theory of contract, based upon the Aristotelian-Thomistic doctrine of commutative justice, which was the

---

ment with anyone to neglect those duties which bind a man to God or to himself."

13. Cf. Leo XIII, *On the Condition of the Working Classes (Rerum novarum)*, ns. 6, 30-31, 54.

14. Cf., *e.g.*, Pius XI, *On Reconstructing the Social Order (Quadragesimo anno)* (New York: Missionary Society of St. Paul, 1939), ns. 116-118; John Paul II, *On Human Work (Laborem exercens)*, ns. 16-17, 19-20, and *On the Hundredth Anniversary of Rerum Novarum (Centesimus annus)* (Washington, D.C.: United States Catholic Conference, 1991), n. 15.

project both of the (Catholic) late-scholastics and northern (Protestant) natural lawyers. His argument suggests that the commutative theory makes better sense of how contemporary courts actually rule than do the courts' own, frequently strained, opinions.

Edwin Epstein's response, "Equity *contra* Inequality," argues that the complexities of the market system inevitably generate disparities—in knowledge, "bargaining power," *etc.*—between contracting parties. Equity as fairness (in the common sense) must, as a practical matter, be restored from without market mechanisms. This, he argues, has been—and must probably continue to be—the role of the courts, even at the expense of wholly consistent legal reasoning.

III

No principle of Catholic social thought has been maintained more consistently, or more insistently, than the Thomistic principle that goods in property are the objects *of* private possession *for* common use;[15] or, in the usage John Paul II prefers, that all property, however held, participates in a *universal destination,*[16] or (following *Gaudium et spes*) answers to a *common purpose.*[17] The organizing teaching of Catholic social thought on work, the just wage, is unintelligible apart from this common use teaching, and the principle of common use itself rests at once upon the very notion of the creation as the Creator's gift to humankind, and upon root principles of distributive and commutative justice. At the same time, it is probably fair to say that no principle of Catholic social thought strikes the modern—and, in particular, the modern American—ear more strangely, for the combination of the terms "private possession" and "common use" may seem, at the very least, oxymoronic.

What may seem less strange to the modern ear is the proposition that the contemporary, "liberal" account of private property—an obliga-

---

15. Cf. Leo XIII, *op. cit.*, ns. 14, 35; Pius XI, *op. cit.*, ns. 45, 47-48; John XXIII, *Mater et Magistra*, ns. 428-429; Paul VI, *Populorum progressio*, ns. 22-24; John Paul II, *On Human Work (Laborem exercens)*, n. 14, who speaks with a blunt emphasis likely to scandalize modern sensibilities: "...*the right to private property is subordinated to the right to common use*..."

16. Cf. John Paul II, *On the Hundredth Anniversary of Rerum Novarum (Centesimus annus)*, IV, ns. 30-31.

17. Cf. Second Vatican Ecumenical Council, Pastoral Constitution on the Church in the World Today, *Gaudium et spes* in *The 16 Documents of Vatican II* (Manila: St. Paul Publications, 1965), ns. 69, 71.

tionless and exclusive right to the possession, use (consumption) and alienation of goods—generates intractable problems for one who looks to justify it philosophically. The contemporary account and its justificatory difficulties provide Thomas Cavanaugh's point of departure in "Aquinas's Account of the Ineradicably Social Character of Private Property." Professor Cavanaugh traces the difficulties to modern conceptual dualism; in the case of property, to the needless introduction of a dichotomy between what one possesses and others' claims to what they urgently need. Thence, he develops St. Thomas's philosophical account of the possession and use of goods from its principles, demonstrating how St. Thomas's account avoids the problematic dichotomies which bedevil the modern account, and issues in an authentically political concept of property, its ownership and its right use.

"The Spirit of Poverty," Wayne Harter's response, grows out of a close consideration of the limits of St. Thomas's philosophical account in the light of his moral theology. If we allow Thomas's theology to complete his philosophy on the question of property, Professor Harter argues, we will find Thomas calling Christians beyond an ethical repose in the legitimacy of ownership and toward a fully religious attitude which, after Paul VI's *Populorum progressio*, he calls "the spirit of poverty." Taken together, Cavanaugh's and Harter's explications of St. Thomas's arguments demonstrate why, in successive social encyclicals, the Popes from Leo XIII to John Paul II have found it sufficient to treat the question of property virtually as a footnote to St. Thomas.

IV

From *Rerum novarum* forward, arguments for the just wage have figured as the practical centerpiece of Catholic social teaching on work and the worker.[18] Moreover, from *Rerum novarum* forward, criticism of the just wage has played variations on a few central themes: prescinding from the question of the soundness of the moral arguments in its favor, how can the just (or living) wage be taken as an imperative in justice if, as seems only too clear, it is practically infeasible—at least, under most (which is to say, the usual) economic circumstances? looking, moreover,

---

18. Thus, *e.g.*, John Paul II, *On Human Work (Laborem exercens)*, n. 19: "...in every case a just wage is the concrete means of *verifying the justice* of the whole socio-economic system..."

at the moral arguments offered in its favor, doesn't the doctrine of the just wage counsel the systematic neglect of simple fairness, for it courts wage-disparities based otherwise than on workers' contributions to the enterprise? again, wouldn't the institutionalization of the just wage lay on business concerns responsibilities which ought to belong either to individual workers or to the agencies of government?

Michael Naughton's essay, "Managers as Distributors of Justice," goes well beyond the conceptual territory suggested by its sub-title, "An Analysis of Just Wages within the Tradition of Catholic Social Thought." Drawing upon contemporary Catholic social teaching on the subjective dimension of work, Professor Naughton looks to make the moral case for the just wage; drawing upon the contemporary literature in strategic human resource management, he looks as well to make the case for the economic feasibility—indeed, for the competitive advantages—of just wage policies. The former undertaking sketches a theory of the firm as a community of workers and managers bound together in solidarity. In the course of the latter undertaking, which is the heart of the essay, Professor Naughton approaches the just wage through its elements—a living wage, an equitable wage, a sustainable wage—showing in each connection how recognized strategic practices can be applied to the achievement, at once, of a just wage-policy and a stronger, more coherent and competitive organization. The essay is notable throughout for its insistence both upon the value and the moral limits of strategic practice, and for its forthright handling of moral and economic objections to the just wage doctrine. Richard Holmberg's response assesses the essay from the perspective of a practicing chief executive officer.

V

"More than ever," John Paul II reminds us, "work is *work with others* and *work for others*;"[19] and the fact of interdependence is a token of the very nature of work:

> [Thus] work bears a particular mark of man and of humanity, the mark of a person operating within a community of persons. And

---

19. *On the Hundredth Anniversary of Rerum Novarum (Centesimus annus)*, n. 31 (emphases original).

this mark decides its interior characteristics; in a sense it constitutes its very nature.[20]

Work's inherently communitarian character goes both to its transitive (or objective) and immanent (or subjective) dimensions. On the one hand:

> Work understood as a "transitive" activity, that is to say an activity beginning in the human subject and directed towards an external object, presupposes a specific dominion by man over "the earth," and in its turn confirms and develops this dominion.... [T]his *process* is...*universal*: it embraces all human beings, every generation, every phase of economic and cultural development, and *at the same time* it is a process that takes place within *each human being*, in each conscious human subject.... Each and every individual, to the proper extent and in an incalculable number of ways, takes part in the giant process whereby man "subdues the earth" through his work.[21]

The process in question, a process which, as John Paul insists, responds to an ordering in the Creator's command: Be fruitful, multiply and fill the earth and subdue it,[22] may also be described as the great, "working" enterprise by which the social organism is cultivated and that aspect of the common human purpose—or good—which consists in the satisfaction of human need is achieved. From the common gift of the Creator, through common enterprise, to a purpose common, because distributive: this, according to John Paul II, is the "particular mark" of work in the objective sense.

On the other hand:

> Man has to subdue the earth and dominate it, because as the "image of God" he is a person, that is to say, a subjective being capable of acting in a planned and rational way, capable of deciding about himself, and with a tendency to self-realization. *As a person, man is therefore the subject of work.* As a person he works, he performs various actions belonging to the work process; independently of their objective content, these actions must all serve to realize his human-

---

20. John Paul II, *On Human Work (Laborem exercens)*, Greeting (p. 5).
21. *Ibid.*, n. 4 (emphases original).
22. Cf. *ibid.*

ity, to fulfill the calling to be a person that is his by reason of his very humanity.[23]

That work is a mode of fulfilling the human vocation, that it is in itself a human good, founds

> ...the strong and deep conviction that man's work concerns not only the economy, but also and especially personal values. The economic system itself and the production process benefit precisely when these personal values are fully respected. In the mind of St. Thomas Aquinas, this is the principal reason in favor of private ownership of the means of production.[24]

John Paul II's reference is to *Summa Theologiae* IIa IIae Q. 66, a. 2. There, St. Thomas discusses how private possession of the fruits of work serves, through the moral and political virtue of owners, to render their use common. Above other justifications, he raises this one: ownership enables the speedy and ready communication of goods to those who are in need of them. The "personal values" to which John Paul II refers, then, are not merely "private" values,[25] but are the values of developed personhood, *e.g.*: justice, generosity, compassion, magnanimity. They are, that is, truly common goods, those which can be held or exercised only in common, only in community. Work in its subjective dimension, then, is indispensable to the promotion of goods which fulfill the person as such, and in which the higher purposes of community consist.

From its inception in *Rerum novarum*, modern Catholic social teaching has entertained the notion of a virtue whose expression is the harmony of needful activity with the virtues that alone render it humane, of individual with common interest, of economic with ethical and spiritual values, of all that belongs to work's objective dimension with all that belongs to its subjective dimension. In this connection, Leo XIII speaks of (social) friendship: between capital and labor, and among the subordinate associations within civil society;[26] Pius XI refers to "social charity."[27]

---

23. John Paul II, *On Human Work (Laborem exercens)*, n. 6 (emphasis original).
24. *Ibid.*, n. 15.
25. In fact, the Latin text has *"bona personae humanae,"* and would be better translated "goods of (or proper to) the human person" (cf. *Acta Ioannis Pauli PP. II, op. cit.*, p. 617).
26. *On the Condition of the Working Classes (Rerum novarum)*, ns. 28-38, *passim.*
27. *On Reconstructing the Social Order (Quadragesimo anno)*, n. 95; cp. ns. 97, 158.

John Paul II proposes to include and illuminate both in solidarity, "a firm and persevering determination to commit oneself to the common good."[28]

John Paul II's definition, and the intention with which he offers it, initiate the concluding essay of this volume, J. Michael Stebbins's "The Meaning of Solidarity." The definition's parts serve to organize Dr. Stebbins's reflection. He offers to characterize the common good as an ordering of the community to the fulfillment of its members, which includes attention to "an authentic scale of values," and which is realized in action through "patterns of cooperation." Commitment to the common good, Dr. Stebbins suggests, is a matter principally of collaboration in the satisfaction of pressing human needs. This stress on solidarity as action justifies John Paul II in treating it under the category of virtue, that is, as a habit or developed "second nature" growing out of sustained practice, but it is the qualifier "sustained," Dr. Stebbins concludes, which ought to engage our particular attention. For, to sustain in loving action is the work of God the Holy Spirit, whose consolations are, then, the *fons et origo* of solidarity. Dan Cawthon's response, "Solidarity and Mystery," reflects on solidarity as a personal essay at resolving "*the* mystery of life," *viz.*: to find one's life is to lose it, to lose it—for another's sake—is to find it.

* * *

At the outset, we suggested that Catholic social thought consists in the theological and philosophical exploration of the difference wrought by the Incarnation for fundamental human aspirations. The modern affect stresses a certain wisdom on human aspiration: as goes their city, so go the citizens. There is a note of fatality in this wisdom, which reminds us that historic social transformations, to which polities are above all subject, regularly seem to go on over the heads and against the intentions of the human agents concerned in them. Catholic social thought stands to remind us of a contrary—not a contradictory—wisdom, borne in antiquity, including Christian antiquity. That ancient wisdom has it that the commonwealth, its works and affections and the order among them, write large the works and affections and the order of the soul. As go the citizens, so goes their city.

In a work which has already been cited here, and is cited in more than

---

28. *Sollicitudo rei socialis*, n. 38.

one of the essays which follow, Josef Pieper, whose signal contributions to Catholic social thought are many, writes:

> Now, to be a Christian *is* a qualification of being, of the whole of a man's being, and the more he opens himself to it, the more completely will it inform and transform all his faculties, including his intelligence.[29]

Read in the light of the ancient wisdom, Pieper's observation bespeaks the hope that, independently of the tides of history and indifferently to every impersonal "force," a transformative Power works for the good in the secret recesses of the soul, yet is not without visible effect; that as its free works touch first the mind and heart, they will first appear in reflection, then in reflective action, and finally in a renewal of the commonwealth as the community of persons free, and flourishing in solidarity. The essays in this volume are tokens of such hope.

---

29. *Leisure, The Basis of Culture*, p. 165.

1

The Quest for a Balanced Appraisal of Work in Catholic Social Thought[1]

James Bernard Murphy

Men like to work. It's a funny thing, but they do. They may moan about it every Monday morning and they may agitate for shorter hours and longer holidays, but they need to work for their self-respect.

That's just conditioning. People can get used to life without work.
Could you? I thought you enjoyed your work?
That's different.
Why?

Well, it's nice work. It's meaningful. It's rewarding. I don't mean in money terms. It would be worth doing even if one wasn't paid anything at all.

David Lodge, *Nice Work*[2]

Lodge captures well here our conflicting intuitions about work. Often, we see work, if not as a necessary evil, then as a mere instrument for "making a living"; in this mood we may hope for emancipation from work, either as an individual—by, say, winning the lottery—or as a society, by some miracle of automation. At other times, however—perhaps when we contemplate a life devoid of work—we realize that we might

---

1. I have benefitted from the comments of Ernest S. Pierucci, Charles Stinson, Patrick Downey and the participants of the inaugural Henning Institute Conference on *Labor, Solidarity and the Common Good*; I wish also to think my indefatigable research assistant, Kevin Walsh.
2. Cited in Stanley Aronowitz and William DiFazio, *The Jobless Future* (Minneapolis: University of Minnesota Press, 1994), p. 328.

actually enjoy our work, that we value it even apart from the income, status and power it might bring. As we recall the skills we have acquired at work and the pleasure of exercising them—the obstacles we have faced and surmounted, the projects accomplished, the services rendered—we realize that we find in work a unique source of fulfillment; that work, along with friendship, religion, knowledge, play, marriage and so forth, is a basic good of human life. Indeed, if we consider the amount of time many of us devote to our work (far beyond what is needed to earn our keep), and if we compare this to the amount of time we devote to our spouses, to our children, to our friends, to church or beauty or play, we might have to conclude that in practice we have made work, not just one intrinsic good among others, but actually our *summum bonum*.

Our intuitions about work, in short, range from valuing it as a merely instrumental good, to valuing it as one intrinsic good among several, to valuing it as the highest good. As it happens, the history of the philosophical analysis of work reflects and embodies this startlingly diverse range of evaluations. What accounts for the radically diverse and mutually inconsistent appraisals of the value of work? Why is there so little agreement among so many wise people about the value of work? After briefly surveying a range of philosophical views, ancient and modern, on the value of work, I will ask: What is it about work that makes a balanced appraisal of it so rare? Why, in other words, is work so often undervalued as a merely instrumental good, or overvalued as the highest of goods?

At present, conflicting valuations of work are playing out against the background of a remarkable change. We are now witnessing, both in Catholic philosophy generally and in official Catholic social teaching, the emergence of a balanced appraisal of work. Work is now taking its rightful place among, but not above, the other intrinsic goods of human life —including, but not limited to, marriage, play, religion, beauty, knowledge, and friendship.

The Macrocosm: The Aristotelian-Thomistic Tradition and Its Critics³

From roughly 348 B.C. to A.D. 1983, philosophical reflection on work within the Aristotelian-Thomistic tradition had consistently maintained: first, that work has merely instrumental—*i.e.*, lacks intrinsic—value; second, that the good of work is found in the product made and not in the perfection of the maker.⁴ Consider Aristotle's distinction between action (πρᾶξις) and production (ποίησις): For while production has an end other than itself, action cannot; for a good action is its own end.⁵ Aristotle is clearly right here: productive work does have an external end; work is directed to the provision of some product or service. Nevertheless, in addition to serving its external end, might not work also be an end in itself? Could work, perhaps, prove to be intrinsically valuable even though it issues in a product or service? After all, Aristotle allows that some intrinsic goods—intelligence, sight, certain pleasures, honor—may also be instrumentally valuable.

In fine, Aristotle resists the appraisal of work as a more-than-instrumental good: "Where there are ends apart from the actions, it is in the nature of the products to be better than the activities."⁶ According to Aristotle, what is valuable in production is the product, not the perfection of the producer. On his account, it makes no sense to inquire about the εὐδαιμονία—the happiness, well-being, flourishing—of the worker as such, since εὐδαιμονία is to be found only in activities that are their own end, and never in activities that are even partly instrumental:

> …if some activities are necessary and desirable for the sake of something else, while others are so in themselves, evidently happiness

---

3. In this section of the paper and in the next, I draw freely from my own previous work on the ethics of labor: cf. *The Moral Economy of Labor: Aristotelian Themes in Economic Theory* (New Haven: Yale University Press, 1993) and "A Natural Law of Human Labor," *American Journal of Jurisprudence* 39 (1994), pp. 71-95.

4. I do not suggest that these two theses exhaust the resources of the tradition on the value of work, still less that one cannot employ other aspects of Aristotelian-Thomistic thought in the service of a balanced appraisal of work (indeed, my *The Moral Economy of Labor* enlists Aristotle to just that end). Nevertheless, these theses present an obstacle to any account of the intrinsic value of work which would claim Aristotelian-Thomistic roots.

5. Aristotle *Nicomachean Ethics* 1140b5 (this and all subsequent citations of Aristotle are from the Revised Oxford Translation, ed. Jonathan Barnes (1984)).

6. *Nicomachean Ethics* 1096b15 and 1094a5.

must be placed in those desirable in themselves, not among those desirable for the sake of something else.[7]

Here, Aristotle's analysis of goods is clearly derived from his metaphysical distinction between immanent and transitive activities (*vide, e.g., Metaphysics* 1050a30). Immanent activities, such as seeing, contemplating, experiencing joy, are complete in themselves; by contrast, transitive activities, such as making and dieting, are incomplete until they reach a goal distinct from the activity itself. From this metaphysical premise, Aristotle draws the normative conclusion that, although some immanent activities have intrinsic value, all transitive activities have only instrumental value. As to work, for Aristotle it is a transitive activity directed to something external to the agent; moral action, by contrast, is an immanent activity perfective of the agent. Only what is perfective of an agent can be an opportunity for flourishing. That work is not perfective —is, indeed, destructive—of the agent is evident when Aristotle comments that if we had automated looms, we would not need slaves.[8] Intrinsically valuable activities—friendship, play, philosophy—are those of which we would deem it odd to wish they were performed for us by slaves or automata.

Curiously, although Aristotle explicitly says, at several junctures, that moral action is "its own end"—that is, is an intrinsic good—he argues in the *Politics* that political and military action are actually but means to a still higher good, to the only good that is complete in and of itself, theoretical speculation. When he says, then, that occupation (ἀσχολία) is a means to leisure (σχολή), he means that both production and action must be directed to, and subordinated to, the really intrinsic good of leisurely speculation.[9]

Thomas Aquinas follows Aristotle, arguing that productive labor, since it aims at the perfection of an external thing, is not an intrinsic good;

---

7. *Ibid.*, 1076b1.

8. Cf. *Politics* 1253b36.

9. On political and military activities as unleisurely occupations (ἀσχολίαι), cf., *e.g., Nicomachean Ethics* 1177b8, and on θεωρία as the one, truly leisurely and complete good, cf. *ibid.* 1177b20; on occupation (ἀσχολία) as a means to leisure (σχολή), cf. *Politics* 1333a35 and 1337b34. "Leisure is a different matter: we think of it as having in itself intrinsic pleasure, intrinsic happiness, intrinsic felicity. Happiness of this order does not belong to those who are engaged in occupation: it belongs to those who have leisure" (*Politics* 1338a1).

moral action, by contrast, is an intrinsic good, because it involves the perfection of the agent.

> The value of an art lies in the thing produced rather than in the artist, since art is right judgment about works to be made. The action of making passes into external material, and is a perfection of the thing made, not of the maker.[10]

Aquinas also follows Aristotle by arguing that production is a transitive activity that perfects an object, whereas action is an immanent activity that perfects an agent.[11]

Among contemporary Thomists, the traditional denial that work has intrinsic value is slowly giving way to a new and more generous appraisal of work, but the traditional orthodoxy remains pervasive. For example, Josef Pieper says baldly: "We work in order to have leisure."[12] And Yves Simon agrees that "...manual work is a useful, not a terminal, activity."[13]

The transition to a new appraisal of work is evident in the thought of Jacques Maritain. In his *Art and Scholasticism* (1935), he follows Aquinas closely: "Thus making...relates to the good or to the proper perfection, not of the man making, but of the work produced";[14] and in *Education at the Crossroads* (1943), he follows Aristotle closely: "... work is not an end in itself; work should afford leisure for the joy, ex-

---

10. *Summa Theologiae* Ia IIae q. 57, a. 5, ad 1.

11. "Producing (*facere*) and acting (*agere*) differ, as stated in the *Metaphysics* [cf. 1050a30], in that producing is an action passing into external matter, thus to build, to saw, and the like; whereas doing is an activity abiding in the agent, thus to see, to will, and the like" (*Summa Theologiae* Ia IIae q. 57. 4c.).

12. Josef Pieper, *Leisure, The Basis of Culture*, trans. Alexander Dru (London: Faber and Faber, 1952), p. 27.

13. Obviously, for Simon, terminal activities are higher than useful activities. Thus, "Work is always useful, forever a means to some end. Contemplation, on the contrary, is always an end in itself, and can thus never be useful. In fact, it is better than useful" (*Work, Society and Culture*, ed. Vukan Kuic (New York: Fordham University Press, 1971), pp. 7, 13).

14. Just as Aristotle said that τέχνη governs ποίησις, while φρόνησις governs πρᾶξις, so Aquinas and Maritain say that art governs making, while prudence governs doing: Prudence works for the good of the one acting, *ad bonum operantis*; Art works for the good of the work made, *ad bonum operis* (cf. Maritain, *Art and Scholasticism*, trans. Joseph W. Evans (New York: Charles Scribner's Sons, 1962), pp. 8, 15). M. D. Chenu sees a more dialectical relation between the perfection of the work and the perfection of the worker. "In the continual interaction of the perfecting of the work and the perfecting of the worker, the former dominates the latter." Chenu goes on to observe, "...the activity of work is still the normal vehicle for man's perfection or his undoing" (*The Theology of Work*, trans. Lilian Soiron (Chicago: Henry Regnery, 1966), pp. 27, 51).

pansion and delight of the spirit."[15] But by 1957 we find Maritain affirming a more modern view of the intrinsic value of work: "The principle of the dignity and human value of manual work is now in the process of being at last realized by human consciousness."[16]

Similarly, until 1983, Germain Grisez and John Finnis excluded work from their lists of the basic goods of human life.[17] Still, change is afoot, even in the *philosophia perennis*: since 1983, Grisez and Finnis have begun to list work as one of the basic, or intrinsic, goods of life, one of the fundamental components of human happiness.[18]

There is a curious parallel between the Aristotelian-Thomistic account of the utility of work and the account offered by modern economics. Economic orthodoxy defines work, not as a good, but as a "bad," what the economists call a disutility: as Alfred Marshall put it, a person's desire to work is measured "...by the sum [of money] which is just required to induce him to undergo a certain fatigue."[19] The logic of treating labor as a disutility was developed beautifully by David Ricardo, who, with his usual bluntness, wrote in 1819 that the level of employment in an economy is of no consequence, so long as rent and profits, out of which flow its new investment, are undiminished. In response, the socialist, Simonde de Sismondi, exclaimed:

> Indeed, wealth is everything, men are absolutely nothing? In truth, then, there is nothing more to wish for than that the king, remaining alone on the island, by constantly turning a crank, might produce, through automata, all the output of England.[20]

---

15. Jacques Maritain, *Education at the Crossroads* (New Haven: Yale University Press, 1943), p. 89.

16. Jacques Maritain, "Some Typical Aspects of Christian Education" (1957), in Donald and Idella Gallagher, eds., *The Education of Man: The Educational Philosophy of Jacques Maritain* (Westport, Connecticut: The Greenwood Press, 1976), p. 149. I am grateful to Ernest Pierucci for bringing this passage to my attention.

17. Cf. Germain Grisez and Russell Shaw, *Beyond the New Morality* (Notre Dame: University of Notre Dame Press, 1974), p. 69, and John Finnis, *Natural Law and Natural Rights* (Oxford: Clarendon Press, 1980), p. 90.

18. For an exploration of the significance of this new development, cf. Murphy, *op. cit.* (1994).

19. Cited in Robert Lane, *The Market Experience* (Cambridge: Cambridge University Press, 1991), p. 265. Some contemporary labor economists concede that people work, not just for the pay, but also for some vaguely characterized set of enjoyments called "work conditions"; the latter seem to amount to social life on the job.

20. Cf. Robert Heilbroner's introduction to Jeremy Rifkin, *The End of Work* (New York: G. P. Putnam's Sons, 1995), p. xi.

Sismondi's nightmare was, more or less, Aristotle's dream.

The new appraisal of the value of work, the appreciation of its importance to human flourishing, emerged first in the Scottish Enlightenment, it seems, and was taken up and deepened in German Romanticism. We do not often value things until they are threatened, and it is noteworthy that the first profound insights into the intrinsic value of work came only when many highly skilled trades had been fragmented into degrading routines by the industrial revolution. Observing how the degradation of labor caused a stultification of the laborers, Adam Ferguson and Adam Smith came to appreciate the unique value of skilled work in perfecting the character and intellect of workers:

> ...the understandings of the greater part of men are necessarily formed by their ordinary employments. The man whose life is spent in performing a few simple operations, of which the effects, too, are, perhaps, always the same, or very nearly the same, has no occasion to exert his understanding, or to exercise his invention in finding out expedients for removing difficulties which never occur. He naturally loses, therefore, the habit of such exertion and generally becomes as stupid and ignorant as it is possible for a human creature to become.[21]

What Smith is saying is that work affords a unique opportunity for self-actualization, but one that can be squandered or corrupted. Work that challenges us to exercise our capacity for invention, work that develops mental and manual skills, will contribute greatly to our well-being; obversely, work that never poses challenges, that requires no real skills, will cause our mind to atrophy. Thus, Alfred Marshall:

> For the business by which a person earns his livelihood generally fills his thoughts during by far the greater part of those hours in which his mind is at his best; during them his character is being formed by the way in which he uses his faculties in his work.[22]

Instead of entertaining a dichotomy between immanent action that perfects the acting self and transitive action that perfects the world, Hegel

---

21. Adam Smith, *The Wealth of Nations*, 5.1. Smith goes on to contrast this grim portrait with the varied and more challenging occupations of men in simpler societies, occupations which "...oblige every man to exert his capacity, and to invent expedients for removing difficulties which are continually occurring....Every man has a considerable degree of knowledge, ingenuity, and invention..."

22. Alfred Marshall, *Principles of Economics*, 1.1.

insisted that the self and the world are jointly transformed in the act of labor: *"Die Arbeit bildet."* Marx, famously, developed Hegel's new metaphysics of action into a theory of the person's self-realization through labor:

> By thus acting on the external world and changing it, he at the same time changes his own nature. He develops his slumbering powers and compels them to act in obedience to his sway.[23]

Considerable empirical evidence supports Ferguson, Smith, Hegel and Marx in the view that work can be morally and intellectually perfective of workers. In a landmark series of studies, for example, Melvin Kohn and Carmi Schooler have clearly demonstrated the profound role of work in either promoting or stunting intellectual growth. By carefully testing the intellectual capacities of a group of men in 1964, then again in 1974, and by measuring the complexity of their job-tasks, Kohn and Schooler found that the cognitive capacities of men with complex jobs developed through their work, while the cognitive capacities of men with simple and repetitive jobs deteriorated.[24] Adam Smith's supposition that a worker "... whose whole life is spent performing a few simple operations...generally becomes as stupid and ignorant as it is possible for a human creature to become" has now been empirically verified. After surveying a vast quantity of literature on industrial psychology, Robert Lane concludes:

> ...working activities are the best agents of well-being and the best sources of cognitive development, a sense of personal control, and self esteem in economic life, better than a higher standard of living, and, I believe, better than what is offered by leisure.[25]

In short, we now have a great deal of evidence not just that people value challenging work, but also that such work is objectively valuable to them.

In response to the crushing burden of more than twenty centuries of philosophical denial of the intrinsic value of work, many modern cham-

---

23. Karl Marx, *Capital* v. I, 7.1.

24. Cf. Melvin Kohn, Carmi Schooler *et al.*, *Work and Personality* (Norwood, New Jersey: Ablex Publishing, 1982), p. 304. "Exercising self-direction in work—doing work that is substantively complex, not being closely supervised, not working at routine tasks—is conducive to favorable evaluations of self, an open and flexible orientation to others, and effective intellectual functioning..." (Melvin Kohn, "Unresolved Issues in the Relationship between Work and Personality," in Kai Erikson, ed., *The Nature of Work* (New Haven: Yale University Press, 1990), p. 42).

25. Robert Lane, *op. cit.*, p. 335.

pions of work were not content merely to insist that work is an intrinsic good, a fundamental opportunity for human flourishing on a par with the other goods of marriage, friendship, play, religion, beauty, knowledge; implicitly or explicitly, rather, they insisted that work is the highest human good. Martin Luther's description of a person's work as his vocation tends to elevate work above, say, play or art, friendship or family. Yet, regarded as distinct and incommensurable goods, play or beauty, knowledge or friendship, are as suitable candidates for a vocation as is work. Similarly, the Protestant work-ethic suggests an unduly privileged status for work, unless accompanied by a play-ethic, a beauty-ethic, a friendship- and marriage-ethic, *etc.*

The Protestant work-ethic yields the anthropology of *homo faber* in, for example, Benjamin Franklin, who first defined man as a tool-making animal. Karl Marx cites Franklin twice, once to poke fun at what he takes to be a characteristically Yankee anthropology, and once with evident approval.[26] Of course, it is no less one-sided to define man as a maker than it was to define him as a knower. *Homo sapiens, homo faber, homo ludens*: man is all these and more. Marx develops his own *homo faber* anthropology, in which work is the principal arena for human self-realization—looking forward in the *Critique of the Gotha Program* to the day when "... labor has become not only a means of life but life's prime want."[27]

But the most explicit and extravagant claims for the superlative value of labor come from Thomas Carlyle, who declares, "It is, after all, the one unhappiness of a man, that he cannot work; that he cannot get his destiny as a man fulfilled."[28] Carlyle emphasized the spiritual value of work: "On the whole, we do entirely agree with those old Monks, *Laborare est Orare*."[29]

Finally, Simone Weil eloquently describes what she takes to be the special place of work in modern spirituality:

Our age has its own particular mission, or vocation—the creation

26. Cf. Jon Elster, *Making Sense of Marx* (Cambridge: Cambridge University Press, 1985), p. 65.

27. Karl Marx, *Critique of the Gotha Program*, I, 3.

28. "All work, even cotton-spinning, is noble; work alone is noble.... Blessed is he who has found his work; let him ask no other blessedness." Cf. Carlyle, *Past and Present* [1843], ed. Richard Altrick (New York: New York University Press, 1977), III, 4 and III, 11.

29. *Ibid.*, III, 12: "All true work is sacred; in all true work, were it but true hand-labor, there is something of divineness."

of a civilization founded upon the spiritual nature of work. The thoughts relating to a presentiment of this vocation, and which are scattered about in Rousseau, George Sand, Tolstoy, Proudhon and Marx, in papal encyclicals and elsewhere, are the only original thoughts of our time, the only ones we haven't borrowed from the Greeks.[30]

Weil rightly points to the radical contrast between ancient and modern appraisals of work, but in denying that work has merely instrumental value, why insist that it is (virtually) the highest good? Shouldn't civilization be built also upon the spiritual nature of play? of beauty and knowledge? marriage and friendship?

L'Entracte: Labor as a *Bonum Arduum*[31]

I know of no other human good whose evaluation by major thinkers ranges from the merely instrumental to the *summum bonum*. Why is a balanced appraisal of work so rarely achieved? I suspect it is because work, paradoxically, is an arduous good, a good that is often experienced as an evil. Every European language has two words for this good, work and labor; and each language uses one of them to convey toil, pain, exertion: πόνος, *labor, Arbeit, travailler*. Don't say to a woman in the pangs of child-birth that labor is a good. Work at its worst ranks among the most inhuman of the cruelties and exploitations known to man: the deliberate destruction of body and spirit through slave-labor, forced labor, child-labor — achieving apotheosis in the Nazi obscenity, "*Arbeit macht frei.*"

The book of Genesis (3:17) treats labor as a punishment for sin: after the fall, work takes on the character of toil. No wonder we all feel at least some degree of disinclination to work. St. Paul did not need to admonish, "He who does not play, enjoy beauty, make friends or marry, neither shall he eat." Even work at its best is an exacting master: when we work, we must submit to a rigorous discipline, to an arduous learning process, to painful exertion. Henri de Man eloquently describes the inescapable elements of toil and pain in work:

---

30. Cited in Alasdair Clayre, *Work and Play* (London: Weidenfield and Nicolson, 1974), p. 1.

31. Pope John Paul II describes work as a *bonum arduum* in his encyclical, *Laborem exercens* (n. 9).

Work inevitably signifies subordination of the worker to remoter aims, felt to be necessary, and therefore involving a renunciation of the freedoms and enjoyments of the present for the sake of a future advantage. Every worker is simultaneously creator and slave.[32]

"And yet," as Pope John Paul II reminds us, "in spite of all this toil — perhaps, in a sense, because of it — work is a good thing for man."[33] From the Christian perspective, of course, the toil and hardship of work have a penitential and redemptive dimension. By enduring the toil of work, each Christian collaborates with the Son of God, carrying his or her daily cross for the redemption of humanity.

But even from a purely philosophical perspective, we can see why the irksomeness of work is inextricably intertwined with the goodness of work. Like all intrinsic goods, work offers a unique mode of human self-realization, albeit a mode considerably less spontaneous and pleasant than that, say, of play. Here, Aristotle's account of the metaphysics of self-realization throws light on the arduous goodness of work. Aristotle emphasizes the priority of act to potency, of activity to passivity, of doing to having. For Aristotle, every virtue — and every intrinsic good — involves the transformation of power ($\delta\acute{v}\nu\alpha\mu\iota\varsigma$) into disposition ($\H{\varepsilon}\xi\iota\varsigma$), and of disposition into activity ($\acute{\varepsilon}\nu\acute{\varepsilon}\rho\gamma\varepsilon\iota\alpha$): human beings flourish by actualizing their potential in the development of complex skills. As John Rawls describes this Aristotelian principle: "Other things being equal, human beings enjoy the exercise of their realized capacities (their innate or trained abilities), and this enjoyment increases the more the capacity is realized, or the greater the complexity."[34] What makes work a fundamental mode of human flourishing is that it affords us the opportunity to develop skills and knowledge from the challenge of solving problems and overcoming obstacles. Meeting the challenges, solving the problems, overcoming the obstacles: all this is difficult, strenuous, frustrating — as well as liberating and rewarding. As Leibniz observed, "*L'inquiétude est essentiel à la félicité des créatures.*" The deep rewards of self-actualization, of the mastery of complex skills, cannot be had but through arduous tedium, the painful exertion of work. The good of work, then, often appears as an evil, because work demands sacrifice in the present for merely possible

---

32. Henri de Man, *Joy in Work*, trans. Eden and Cedar Paul (London: George Allen and Unwin, 1929), p. 67.

33. *Laborem exercens*, n. 9.

34. John Rawls, *A Theory of Justice* (Cambridge: Harvard University Press, 1971), p. 426.

future rewards, and because work brings mastery only if we submit to arduous discipline. Such a paradoxical good is bound to generate conflicting appraisals.

Microcosm: Official Catholic Social Teaching

What we find in official Catholic social teaching over the past century is a recapitulation of the bewildering range of evaluations we noted in the more than twenty centuries of philosophical reflection on work. Even more remarkably, we find in the development of these appraisals the like general pattern: from a merely instrumental good, work rises to an intrinsic good — perhaps to the highest good — and finally settles into a balanced appraisal as one among several intrinsic goods. Thus, official Catholic social teaching appears as a true microcosm of the wider universe of thought on labor.

In the encyclical, *Rerum novarum* (1891), of Pope Leo XIII, we find a very clear and emphatic assertion of the traditional Thomistic view that labor has merely instrumental value. But whereas Aristotle and Thomas treat work principally as a means to an artifact, Leo XIII treats work principally as means to the support of the worker and his family. He declares, "...when a man engages in remunerative labor, the very reason and motive of his work is to obtain property, and to hold it as his own private possession."[35] Indeed, for the Pope, the possession of private property is undoubtedly a higher good than labor.[36] Of course, the mere fact that labor is a means to the acquisition of property does not imply that a laborer can be treated merely as a means to the profit of his employer. Leo XIII denounces the exploitation of workers by their employers with great passion.[37]

In other words, the Pope condemns the degradation of the laborer rather than the degradation of labor. He condemns the long hours, the

---

35. *Rerum novarum*, n. 4. This and all subsequent texts of official Catholic social teaching are drawn from David J. O'Brien and Thomas J. Shannon, eds., *Catholic Social Thought: The Documentary Heritage* (New York: Orbis Books, 1992).

36. Thus, *ibid.*, n. 30: "It must be borne in mind that the chief thing to be secured is the safeguarding, by legal enactment and policy, of private property."

37. *E.g., ibid.*, n. 16: "Religion teaches the rich man and the employer that their work people are not their slaves....that it is shameful and inhuman to treat men like chattels to make money by..."

harsh conditions, the brutal physical exhaustion imposed on men, women and children by rapacious employers.[38] He almost never mentions the degradation of work itself into mindless routine, the imprisonment of each worker in a simple, repetitive task, or the complete separation of the conception of tasks by managers from the execution of those tasks by workers. Such abuses destroy the intrinsic value of work for the worker; they make what could be a self-perfective, into a self-destructive, undertaking. Of course, the degradation of labor through its detailed division ultimately entails the degradation of the laborer, but this consequence is not what Leo XIII condemns. His target is, above all, employers' proclivity to exploit the desperation of poor workers by paying them too little and working them too hard.[39] He does not directly criticize their related proclivity to remove all thought, judgment and discretion from workers, making them into mindless drudges.

To be sure, the Pope teaches, "...there is nothing to be ashamed of in seeking one's bread by labor"—but the fact that labor is not shameful does not make it worthy. On the matter of worth, Leo XIII insists, "...the true dignity of man lies in his moral qualities, that is, in virtue; that virtue is the common inheritance of all, equally within the reach of high and low, rich and poor..."[40] Although many skilled craftsmen might well find in their craft a real source of dignity and virtue, Leo distinguishes labor from the dignity of the moral virtues. As we shall see, one of his successors will claim that labor properly embodies, not just intellectual, but also moral virtue.

Pope Pius XI's *Quadragesimo anno* (1931) generally proceeds on Pope Leo's premise that labor has merely instrumental value. Thus the labor contract, like any exchange, must meet the standard of just price (in this case, just wage); again, the evil of capitalism is identified mainly with exploitative wages, as "...one class is forbidden to exclude the other from a share in the profits."[41] Revealingly, when Pius XI recommends that, where feasible, employers invite employees to become part-owners of a shared enterprise, he seems to do so not by way of enabling workers to

---

38. Cf. *ibid.*, nn. 16, 27, 29, 33, 34.

39. Leo XIII says of the employer (*Rerum novarum*, n. 17), "His great and principal obligation is to give to everyone that which is just.... To defraud anyone of wages that are his due is a crime..."

40. *Rerum novarum*, n. 20.

41. *Quadragesimo anno*, n. 57; for the lengthy analysis of just wages, cf. nn. 56-75.

protect the dignity of their work, but by way of enabling them to secure their fair share of profits.[42]

However, the Pope sows the seeds of a recognition that work may perfect — or degrade — the soul of man; he allows, subtly, that labor may offer an opportunity for human flourishing:

> ... very many employers treated their workmen as mere tools, without any concern for the welfare of their souls.... And so bodily labor, which was decreed by Providence for the good of man's body and soul even after original sin, has everywhere been changed into an instrument of strange perversion: for dead matter leaves the factory ennobled and transformed, where men are corrupted and degraded.[43]

This passage invites an immediate question: What is the source of the degradation the Pope laments? Are workers degraded by the mindless tedium of their tasks, or by the external conditions of work? From the context, it seems that Pius XI here traces the degradation of workers to the sexual license promoted by overcrowded housing and by the mixing of the sexes at work.[44] Hence, we cannot conclude that Pius recognizes the link between the degradation of work itself and the degradation of the worker. Still, whatever its author's intent, this passage will come to fruition, thirty years after its writing, in John XXIII's new appraisal of work.[45]

The first clear recognition of the intrinsic value of work to be found in the series of social encyclicals appears in John XXIII's *Mater et magistra* (1961). At many junctures, Pope John echoes the traditional concern for the just remuneration of labor,[46] but in a few passages he strikes quite a new note. Consider:

---

42. "...we deem it advisable that the wage contract should, when possible, be modified somewhat by a contract of partnership.... For thus the workers and executives become sharers in the ownership or management, or else participate in some way in the profits" (*Quadragesimo anno*, n. 65).

43. *Quadragesimo anno*, n. 135.

44. Thus, *ibid.*: "The mind shudders if we consider the frightful perils to which the morals of workers (of boys and young men particularly), and the virtue of girls and women are exposed in modern factories..."

45. John XXIII cites this passage in *Mater et magistra* (1961), n. 242.

46. *E.g.*, *Mater et magistra*, n. 68, "Our heart is filled with profound sadness when we observe...great masses of workers who, in not a few nations...receive too small a return from their labor"; cf. also, n. 18.

Justice is to be observed not merely in the distribution of wealth, but also in regard to the conditions under which men engaged in productive activity have an opportunity to assume responsibility and to perfect themselves by their efforts.[47]

For the first time, to my knowledge, here is a recognition that work has the intrinsic potential to perfect workers, and that to the degree that a worker has some responsibility for the conception as well as for the execution of his tasks. Indeed, John XXIII goes further and—again, for the first time—condemns as unjust the fragmentation of work into monotonous routines, even if workers are otherwise justly compensated.[48]

Whereas Leo XIII had ascribed to labor the value of an instrument for acquiring property, John XXIII explicitly says that professional skills are more valuable than property: the skills of work shape who we are, while property is merely what we have.[49] At the same time, Pope John recognizes that work is not the only intrinsic good and that provision must be made to free up time for play and family.[50]

John XXIII's reflections on the intrinsic value of work are developed and clarified in the Second Vatican Council's statement, *Gaudium et spes* (1965). Here we find the Hegelian theme of the joint articulation of world and self in the act of labor:

For when a man works he not only alters things and society, he develops himself as well. He learns much, he cultivates his resources, he goes outside of himself and beyond himself.[51]

---

47. *Mater et magistra*, n. 82.

48. *Ibid.*, n. 83, the Pope writes, "...if the human organization and structure of economic life be such that the human dignity of workers is compromised, or their sense of responsibility is weakened, or their freedom of action is removed, then we judge such an economic order to be unjust, even though it produces a vast amount of goods whose distribution conforms to the norms of justice and equity." Moreover, John says (n. 92) that from the need for efficient management "...it by no means follows that those who work daily in...an enterprise are to be considered merely as servants, whose function is to execute orders silently..."

49. Thus, *ibid.*, nn. 106-107: "It sometimes happens in our day that men are more inclined to seek some professional skill than possession of goods....This clearly accords with the inherent characteristics of labor, inasmuch as this proceeds directly from the human person, and hence is to be thought more of than wealth in external goods. These latter, by their very nature, must be regarded as instruments."

50. *Mater et magistra*, n. 250: "...it is right and necessary for man to cease for a time from labor, not merely to relax his body from daily work and likewise to refresh himself with decent recreation, but also to foster family unity..."

51. *Gaudium et spes*, n. 35.

Pope John's elevation of skilled labor above property is reaffirmed:

> ...this kind of growth [from work] is of greater value than any external riches which can be garnered. A man is more precious for what he is than for what he has.[52]

From its observation that work affords a unique opportunity for human flourishing, the Council exhorts employers to design jobs that promote the perfection, rather than the degradation, of workers: "The opportunity should also be afforded to workers to develop their own abilities and personalities through the work they perform..."[53]

In every statement of official Catholic social teaching save one, consideration of the labor process itself, of the intrinsic value and dignity of work, is limited to a few paragraphs scattered through a wide-ranging discussion of many issues in social, political and economic life. In *Laborem exercens* (1981), Pope John Paul II, alone among the modern pontiffs, makes work the focus of an analysis of modern social and economic life.[54] His profound speculative and phenomenological exploration of the meaning of work for modern society represents a radical break with the whole Aristotelian-Thomistic tradition. Indeed, John Paul II's forceful assertion of its high intrinsic value leads him to treat work virtually as the highest human good. He repeatedly insists that work cannot be reduced to an instrument:

> It [labor] is not only good in the sense that it is useful or something to enjoy; it is also good in the sense that it is worthy, that is to say, something that corresponds to man's dignity, that expresses this dignity and increases it.[55]

While Aristotle and Aquinas argue that work is not perfective of man, the Pope insists that work *is* perfective of man. Indeed, in large measure, the Pope adopts Marx's theory of human self-realization through work:

> Work is a good thing for man — a good thing for his humanity — because through work man not only transforms nature, adapting it

---

52. *Ibid.*
53. *Ibid.*, n. 67.
54. Indeed, John Paul claims that "...human work is *a key*, probably *the essential key*, to the whole social question..." (*Laborem exercens*, n. 3).
55. *Laborem exercens*, n. 9.

to his own needs, but he also achieves fulfillment as a human being and indeed, in a sense, becomes "more a human being."[56]

Recall that, for Aquinas, making is governed by craft (*ars*), an intellectual virtue, while acting is governed by prudence, a moral virtue; art works for the good of the thing made, while prudence works for the good of the one acting. John Paul II's radical break with St. Thomas is nowhere more evident than in his bold claim that work stems from a moral virtue[57]—namely, industriousness. This virtue, for John Paul II, involves moral dispositions to patience, perseverance, conscientiousness and efficiency. Work is now taken to be perfective both of man's intellect and of his character.

The burden of *Laborem exercens*, that on the labor process—on work—turns the question of human dignity in the modern era, leads John Paul II to a radical critique of the degradation of labor under both capitalist and communist regimes. For all their differences, both regimes tend to design labor processes that deprive workers of autonomy and discourage their initiative.[58] The Pope challenges employers to design jobs consistent with the principle that "work is for man, man is not for work."[59] Work is for man in the sense that the subjective dignity of the worker—not the pay, nor the productivity, nor the value added—is the measure of work. To be *for man*, work must be designed to respect each worker's capacity for self-direction and self-development. Instead of seeking to habituate workers to the degrading tedium of their jobs—jobs too small for the human spirit—we must seek to redesign jobs as vehicles of the human quest for self-realization.[60]

---

56. *Ibid.*, n. 7. As John Finnis said to me in conversation, had the Pope been a better Thomist, he never would have written *Laborem exercens*.

57. Apart from recognizing that, through work, man becomes "more a human being," John Paul writes, "It is impossible to understand the virtue of industriousness, and more particularly it is impossible to understand why industriousness should be a virtue: for virtue, as a moral habit, is something whereby man becomes good as man" (*Laborem exercens*, n. 9). For St. Thomas, by contrast, *industria*—far from being a moral virtue—was the amoral capacity for cleverness (Aristotle's δεινότης), a capacity employable indifferently for good or evil; cf. *Summa Theologiae* Ia IIae q. 21, a. 2 ad 2, and IIa IIae q. 47, a. 13 ad 3.

58. On John Paul II's comparison of the degradation of labor under capitalism and communism, cf. *Laborem exercens*, n. 13.

59. *Laborem exercens*, n. 6.

60. *Ibid.*, n. 7: "Man is treated as an instrument of production, whereas he—he alone, independent of the work he does—ought to be treated as the effective subject of work and its true maker and creator."

Like other champions of the value of work, John Paul II tends to appraise work as the highest — one might almost say, the only — human good. He begins *Laborem exercens* by extending the name "work" to "…any activity by man, whether manual or intellectual, whatever its nature or circumstances…" But so expansive a usage makes every human activity, even play, a kind of work. Even though we often say that we are "working" on our marriage, or on a friendship, we also understand that the activities whereby we enjoy such goods as marriage, play or friendship hardly qualify as work. Aristotle and Aquinas are right to insist that work, as work, has a transitive dimension, that it must be directed, at least in part, to an external result. Not all human activities are kinds of work, and neither are all human goods the good of work.

John Paul II asserts that "…from work it [man's life] derives its specific dignity" and that "human work is *a key*, probably *the essential key*, to the whole social question…."[61] But such claims could, just as plausibly, be made on behalf of other intrinsic goods, on behalf of marriage or friendship, for example, or on behalf of religion. Moreover, the Pope claims that, in a way, "work is a condition for making it possible to found a family" and that "work and industriousness also influence the whole process of education in the family…."[62] These claims suggest that work is the necessary precondition for enjoyment of the other goods of human life, which may be true in an economic sense, but hardly in a logical sense. Finally, John Paul claims, "Man must work both because the Creator commanded it and because of his humanity, which requires work in order to be maintained and developed."[63] Of course, if every human activity proves to be a kind of work, this claim is true, but trivial; if, however, work is but one of several intrinsic, incommensurable human goods, then the claim is misleadingly one-sided.

John Paul II also develops a theology and spirituality of work in *Laborem exercens*. Central to both is the principle, "Man, created in the image of God, shares by his work in the activity of the Creator…."[64] True, even profoundly true; but man shares in the activity of God through all of the intrinsic goods of human life. The Pope's theology of work centers around an analogy between God's creation and human production: by working, we share in God's creative activity. Is God's creation of the

---

61. *Laborem exercens*, nn. 1, 3.
62. *Ibid.*, n. 10.
63. *Ibid.*, n. 16.
64. *Laborem exercens*, n. 25.

world out of nothing analogous to craftsman's imposition of form on matter? Augustine thought not:

> By what means did you make heaven and earth? What tool did you use for this vast work? You did not work as a human craftsman does, making one thing out of something else as his mind directs.... Nor did you have in your hand any matter from which you could make heaven and earth, for where could you have obtained matter which you had not yet created, in order to use it as material for making something else?[65]

Again, it seems just as plausible to suppose that we participate in God's creative activity through marital procreation, or even through play. John Paul II's theology, like his philosophy, of work—though full of marvelous insights—ultimately lacks balance.

List des heiligen Geistes?

Still, nothing succeeds like excess. There is reason to believe that it took John Paul II's sometimes extravagant argument for the intrinsic value of work to defeat the Thomistic orthodoxy. Even after the rather strong claims made on behalf of work's intrinsic value in *Mater et magistra* and *Gaudium et spes*, major Catholic philosophers were still omitting work from their lists of intrinsic goods, of basic opportunities for human flourishing.[66] After the very forceful restatement of Church teaching in *Laborem exercens*, these philosophers quietly revised their lists to include work.[67]

After more than twenty centuries of evaluations—ranging from mere instrument to *summum bonum*—we now witness for the first time, in the wake of *Laborem exercens*, the emergence of a balanced appraisal of work, both in the wider Aristotelian-Thomistic tradition and in official Catholic social teaching. Philosophers Germain Grisez and John Finnis now rank work as one among several intrinsic, incommensurable human goods. The American bishops, in their pastoral letter on the economy

---

65. Augustine *Confessions*, XI 5. The Hebrew word for God's creative activity (*bara*) is carefully distinguished in the Scriptures from the words for human production.

66. Cf. Grisez and Shaw, *loc. cit.*, and Finnis, *loc. cit.*

67. Cf. Germain Grisez, *Christian Moral Principles* v. I (1983), p. 124, and G. Grisez, Joseph Boyle and John Finnis, "Practical Principles, Moral Truth, and Ultimate Ends," *American Journal of Jurisprudence* 32 (1987), p. 107.

(1986), after affirming John Paul II's teaching on the intrinsic value of work, add this subtle, but crucial, corrective: "Leisure, prayer, celebration, and the arts are also central to the realization of human dignity and to the development of a rich cultural life."[68]

Thus, in both the wider currents of philosophical reflection and the narrower stream of official Catholic social teaching, we find a parallel development in the appraisal of work: from merely instrumental good, to highest human good, to one among several intrinsic goods. Astonishing is that these parallel developments converge — again, in the wake of *Laborem exercens* — on a remarkably balanced appraisal of work. Such a convergence, and the achievement of such an appraisal, are signs of hope for our times.

---

68. U.S. Catholic Conference, *Economic Justice for All* (1986), n. 96.

Homo Reflectens:
A Response to James B. Murphy

Patrick Downey

In the light of Professor Murphy's paper, and of the other papers presented here, I feel a bit like Diogenes at the siege of Corinth. When asked by the citizens of the city why he was trundling his tub back and forth across the square while the rest of the city prepared for war, he replied that he did not want to be the only idler among so many industrious citizens. Industrious Professor Murphy's paper certainly is, and I have little to add to his erudition and thoroughness, apart from a few — perhaps, trifling — rolls of my own tub.

Perhaps I should begin with the simple, central word — "balanced." When I think of balance, two images come to mind. One is that of mathematical masses opposed to one another on either side of a fulcrum: when both masses are equal, as measured by the abstract quantity of weight, the system has achieved balance. The second image is that of a gymnast, who is balanced so far as she can do all of her jumps and stands without a fall or misstep. Professor Murphy impressively brings out the parallel development through which the macrocosmic philosophical, and microcosmic Church, teachings on work have converged, and he notes — with some satisfaction — the additions this change has stimulated in the moral philosophies of Finnis and Grisez. What I question, however, is whether this movement in the realm of philosophy, on the one hand, and of Catholic social thought, on the other, has been a development between opposed extremes, leading to a healthy balance in the middle. Might it, instead, be a case of having lost one's feet, and taken that extra step that indicates balance has, in fact, been lost?

Consider what is, perhaps, only a comment Professor Murphy has made in passing, but one which has immense implications for his notion of balance.

> Of course, it is no less one-sided to define man as a maker than it was to define him as a knower. *Homo sapiens, homo faber, homo ludens*: man is all these and more.

Man is indeed all of these, but the question is whether he can be defined by all of them. For, a definition is adequate only if it succeeds at including within itself—by implication and essentially—all other characteristics, only if it functions as a higher, ordering principle in relation to lower, ordered attributes.

Again, as to *homo sapiens, homo faber, homo ludens,* and so on: it is because we can "know" that we can "play" and "make," but being able to make is no guarantee that we can also know. As Nietzsche saw clearly, if we are defined by our making, our "creativity," all we can ever know is our own fictions—not the truth, and certainly not reality. In other words, *homo sapiens* "balances" *homo faber,* because knowing makes sense of our making. Man the maker, on the other hand, cannot balance himself, for he cannot make sense of his knowing and so must always reduce it to something else. Balance, therefore, is not a question of avoiding being "one-sided," but is a question of keeping one's feet—and one's head—of getting it essentially right; only then is one truly able to order the details.

All of this brings us to the two famous definitions of the human given by Aristotle: man as the "rational animal," and man as the "political animal." Professor Murphy, once again, has done a fine job of bringing out the implications of the first definition for the early account of work in subordination to σχολή, or the leisure of rational contemplation. What he has, perhaps, neglected—yet, it is ultimately indispensable for balancing the more ancient against the modern appraisals of work—is the role of the political. For, when we see Aristotle define politics as the architectonic science, we can see as well that τέχνη—the knowledge of how to make or work well—must have its first principles outside itself in the architectonic knowing of politics. Τέχνη, as the knowledge "how" to make something, does indeed have its goal—hence, its good—outside itself in the product made; still, as a mode of knowing in a rational knower, it is also intrinsically tied into what the maker is as a human being. The way this connection between the maker and knower is itself forged is not found by looking to what is made, but rather to *why* it is made. For the question, why make and work on "this" rather than "that," the question of ordering an entire πολιτεία—a whole political community, including within itself both an economy and a culture—is the question that demands a political answer. So, for better or worse, it is with politics that we must seek out the meaning, worth, intrinsic value of the worker and his work.

Now, to raise the political question is to return ourselves to the Aristotelian-Thomistic universe, for the answers implicit in our working, that give working its intrinsic worth even while it is oriented towards an extrinsic end or product, can be examined and weighed only through a theoretical grasp of our essential nature as human beings. Is that nature something we have made through our history and the "spiritual work" of civilization? If so, we are at bottom our own gods, and our work is the labor of God absent the seventh day of rest and leisure. If we have not created our own nature, then our desire to know—to know the whole, ourselves, how we ought, politically and ethically, to order our work and our leisure—is itself the reflexively essential activity wherein we are most ourselves. In other words, *only* if we are *not* the makers of our own nature are we free to rest in ourselves, even in the midst of our greatest labor; for then it is us—the worker, rather than the work—that makes whatever we do worth the doing.

There is no need to dispute the claims for the power of interesting work to help make life worth the living of it for most people; but the cause of this effect lies not in production as such, but in the rational activity of the worker who, even in merely knowing "how" to produce something, exercises his intrinsic nature as a *knower*, rather than a maker. It is the "more" the worker must know that increases his satisfaction in his work, but even the most satisfying work of, say, the nuclear engineer, raises the further question whether one should indulge in such satisfactions. The satisfactions of work are, therefore, tied into the higher question of politics, and the ἀρχὴ in the architectonic question of politics is the first principle of our human nature. How does it fit into the rest of nature at large? However we are to uncover this nature, the one thing we can sure of is that the end of inquiry will not be something we make, but must be something we find. Moreover, however industrious we may be in pursuit of that discovery, only in the realm of leisure—of σχολὴ and the rest of the seventh day—can it possibly be made.

Professor Murphy's balanced appraisal, whereby work takes "its rightful place among, but not above, the other intrinsic goods of human life—including, but not limited to, marriage, play, religion, beauty, knowledge and friendship," will thus be no balance at all, unless it finds the true principle of balance that does not merely lay out human goods side by side, but puts them in motion in the life of human being who, in knowing himself, knows what he is doing. Only as rational and political animals can we seek out and judge what work is worth doing, how we are to do it, and why we are able—oftentimes—to find such joy in it.

2

Labor and Commutative Justice

James Gordley

Labor is not merely a matter of contract, and justice to those who labor is not merely contractual justice. Labor, like all human activities, is a realization of one's human potential. It is a particularly important one, since it is what most people do most of their lives, and a primary way in which they use their human capacities to plan, to build and to serve. Moreover, labor is the way most people support themselves, and therefore the earnings from labor matter from the standpoint of distributive justice. Nevertheless, most often, labor is provided and rewarded through a contract. Earnings are spent by making further contracts to buy what one needs. Here, I would like to consider contractual justice.

Much of the unfairness that Upton Sinclair depicted in his book, *The Jungle*, was contractual injustice. Not all of it, certainly: he described how work could frustrate the achievement of one's human potential. One need only think of the boy, Stanislaus,

> [h]our after hour, year after year,...stand[ing] on a certain square foot of floor...making never a motion and thinking never a thought save for the setting of lard cans.[1]

He described the appalling, low level of wages, a level which he thought was artificially maintained by luring immigrants into areas where there was not sufficient work for them.[2] Still, Sinclair's protagonists suffered time and again, because of the contracts they made.

First, everything they bought was defective: their dilapidated house, perched over a cesspool containing the drainage of fifteen years; the pale-blue milk, doctored with formaldehyde; the canned peas and fruit jams,

---

1. Upton Sinclair, *The Jungle* (N.Y.: Bantam Books, 1981), p. 71.
2. Sinclair, *op. cit.*, p. 66.

colored with copper salts and aniline dyes.[3] Next, their jobs put their lives and health at serious risk. The image that moved the American public most was that of men falling into unfenced vats of boiling meat.[4] Finally, they had no job security: they could be fired for any reason or no reason. They could, therefore, be plunged into abject poverty at any moment.

Sinclair judged these injustices to be inherent in an economic system based on contract. To try to end them, his protagonist became a socialist. Indeed, Sinclair's illustrations were chosen to show that injustice is inevitable when the rights of workers are based on private contracts. We can see his point when we consider the contract law of his time. According to most jurists, whether a contract was fair or unfair was a matter for its parties themselves to consider. It was no concern of the courts. Each of Sinclair's examples of contractual injustice was an instance in which the courts had refused to help, supposedly, because it was up to the contracting party to help himself.

In the case of defective products, the traditional rule had been *caveat emptor*, "Let the buyer beware." If the buyer wanted protection against defects, it was up to him to ask the seller to warrant them in the contract. Absent a warranty, the buyer was protected only against fraud. Fraud, moreover, meant telling a lie: for example, it meant falsely denying that the goods were defective. Silence about a defect did not constitute fraud.

Similarly, the law of the time did not protect a worker against unsafe conditions absent an express provision in the contract. If the worker knew the job site was dangerous, it was up to him to refuse to work there unless the site was made safe. If he continued to work, he would be held to be contributorily negligent, or to have assumed the risk of getting hurt. Consequently, the clearer the danger, the worse the position of the worker, since the clearer it was that he knew of it. A worker at the American Axe and Tool Company once complained to his boss that the rack that held the hatchets he was painting was loose. Oliver Wendell Holmes, then on the Massachusetts Supreme Court, held that the worker could not recover when a hatchet fell on him, since he knew of the danger and yet stayed on the job.[5]

Again, the law of Sinclair's time—and indeed, as we will see, sometimes the law of our own—did not provide security of employment absent an express provision in the contract. An employment contract was

3. *Ibid.*, p. 75.
4. *Ibid.*, p. 99.
5. Lamson v. American Axe & Tool Co., 58 N.E. 585 (Mass. 1900).

terminable at will, by either party, for any reason or for no reason. If an employee wanted job security, it was up to him to provide for it in the contract.

The question I want to consider here is not so much whether these results are unjust as why they might be. We need a theory of contract that explains why the terms of a contract can be unfair. In part, results such as these were tolerated because, in the 19th and early 20th centuries, fairness was not supposed to be an integral part of contract law. Whether the terms of a contract were fair was for the parties to worry about, not the courts. Joseph Story, a Supreme Court Justice and professor at the Harvard Law School, had explained:

> [E]very person who is not from his peculiar condition under disability is entitled to dispose of his property as he chooses; and whether his bargains are wise and discreet or profitable or unprofitable or otherwise are considerations not for courts of justice but for the party himself to deliberate upon.[6]

Story's views were an early American expression of what we now call a "will theory" of contract. In the 19th century, Western jurists defined contract as the expression of the will of the parties to be bound.[7] The novel feature of this theory was not the idea that people make contracts by expressing their will to be bound; jurists had always known that contracts are entered into voluntarily. The novelty, as A.W.B. Simpson has noted, is that the will was regarded as a kind of *Grundnorm* from which all the parties' obligations were supposed to derive.[8] Thus, the very con-

---

6. Joseph Story, *Commentaries on Equity Jurisprudence as Administered in England and America*, 14th ed., v. 1 (Boston, 1918), p. 337.

7. Cf., *e.g.*, Christopher C. Langdell, *A Summary of the Law of Contracts*, 2nd ed. (Boston, 1880), pp. 1-21; Stephen Leake, *Elements of the Law of Contracts* (London, 1867), pp. 7-8; Frederick Pollock, *Principles of Contract: Being a Treatise on the General Principles Concerning the Validity of Agreements in the Law of England*, 4th ed. (London, 1885), pp. 1-9; Charles Demolombe, *Cours de Code Napoléon*, v. 24 (Paris, 1854-82), § 12; Léon Larombière, *Théorie et pratique des obligations*, v. 1 (Paris, 1857), § 41; François Laurent, *Principes de droit civil français*, 3rd ed., v. 15 (Paris, 1878-96), §§ 424-27; Georg Friedrich Puchta, *Pandekten*, 2nd ed. (Berlin, 1844), §§ 49, 54; Friedrich Carl von Savigny, *System des heutigen römischen Rechts*, v. 3 (Berlin, 1840-48), § 134; Bernhard Windscheid, *Lehrbuch des Pandektenrechts*, 7th ed., v. 1 (Frankfort-on-Main, 1891), § 69. *See generally*, James Gordley, *The Philosophical Origins of Modern Contract Doctrine* (Oxford, 1991), pp. 161-213.

8. A.W.B. Simpson, "Innovation in Nineteenth Century Contract Law," *Law Quarterly Review* 91 (1975), 247 at 266.

ception of contract law seemed to require a court to ask, not what contractual terms would be fair, but what terms the parties had provided for themselves.

By the end of the 19th century, one obvious difficulty with this theory had been detected. Whenever the parties have not resolved a problem expressly in their contract, the law must resolve it one way or another. It is no good saying that one party could have insisted on a term to cover the matter, for the other party could have done so as well. And, in fact, the law is always reading terms into contracts when the parties were silent, and indeed, when they never thought about the matter. If you order furniture and agree only on the items and the price, the law of sales governs all the questions you have left open; if you rent a house, the questions left open are governed by the law of leases, and so forth. It is hard to see how the will of the parties can be the source of these obligations.

Some European jurists claimed that will was the source of all the parties' obligations without explaining how that could be.[9] Others said that the law merely supplied the terms that the parties would have thought of themselves. The function of the law was simply "to dispense the parties from writing them into their instruments..."[10] Other jurists admitted that the parties probably would not have thought of all these terms themselves, but insisted that the parties willed their obligations to be those the law would read into their contract. At the turn of the century, one critic offered the caricature: "Question, what does the law will? Answer: what the parties will. What do the parties will? What the law wills!"[11]

In the United States, considerations like these led Oliver Wendell Holmes and Samuel Williston to reject the will theories in favor of a so-called "objective theory" of contract.[12] According to an "objective theory," the terms the law reads into a contract have nothing to do with the will of the parties. The law simply puts them there. One weakness of this theory is that it does not explain why the law supplies one set of terms rather than another. This weakness may explain why, eventually, most American jurists became disillusioned with the objective theory. For present purposes, we need only note that, in one respect, the objective the-

---

9. Puchta, *Pandekten*, § 58.

10. Laurent, *Principes* 16, § 182.

11. Siegmund Schlossmann, review of Ernst Zitelmann, *Irrthum und Rechtsgeschäft*, *Zeitschrift für das Privat- und öffentliche Recht der Gegenwart* 7 (1980), p. 562.

12. Oliver Wendell Holmes, Jr., "The Path of the Law," in O. W. Holmes, Jr., *Collected Legal Papers* (New York, 1920), pp. 177-79; Samuel Williston, *The Law of Contracts*, v. 2 (New York, 1920), §§ 20, 605-08, 615.

ory and the will theory were much alike. In neither theory did terms belong to a contract because the terms were fair. Neither group of theorists thought that one could analyze whether terms were fair.

We can see, then, why Upton Sinclair thought he was not merely exposing the dishonesty of the Chicago meat packers, but was indicting an economic system based on contract. Contract meant that those who did not protect themselves would be treated unfairly. This idea became a staple among reformers in the early 20th century. In his 1903 book, *Studies in the Evolution of Industrial Society*, Richard Ely argued that only on the assumption that people are equal can "each one guard his own interests individually, providing only the hampering fetters of law should make way for a reign of liberty." But in reality:

> back of the contract lies inequality in strength of those who form the contract.... Wealth and poverty, plenty and hunger, nakedness and warm clothing, ignorance and learning, face each other in contract, and find expression in and through contract.[13]

These arguments were tracked by Roscoe Pound in his famous 1909 essay, "Liberty of Contract."[14] For both Ely and Pound, they explained why there had to be less contract and more state intervention.

Through the efforts of the reformers, some of the unjust practices that Sinclair exposed were eventually remedied. Nevertheless, the reformers were better at enlisting support to remedy them than they were at explaining why these practices were unjust and in need of a remedy. Indeed, their critique of contract law was constructed on the very premises of the will theorists. The law of contract merely enforced whatever the parties agreed upon, whether fair or not. Since contract law did not protect the parties against unfairness, and since the parties often could not protect themselves, the state had to do so. This account of contract does not tell us when a particular term of a contract is unfair any more than the will theories and objective theories. Unfairness is simply what happens when one party is stronger than another.

Today, whatever the injustices we have managed to remedy, we still lack a theory of what would make a contract just or unjust. I would like to describe a theory that purported to do exactly that. It had been widely

---

13. Richard Ely, *Studies in the Evolution of Industrial Society* (New York, 1903), p. 402.
14. Roscoe Pound, "Liberty of Contract," *Yale Law Journal* 18 (1909), p. 454.

held among jurists before the 19th century. It fell from favor with the rise
of the will theories. A discussion of this theory is particularly appropriate for this conference, since one of its original architects was Saint
Thomas Aquinas. I first will describe the theory, then discuss how it
might apply to Sinclair's examples of unjust contracts.

Thomas Aquinas developed this theory on the basis of ideas he took
from Aristotle.[15] His work was then further elaborated in the 16th century by a group of theologians, philosophers and jurists centered in Spain,
and known to historians as the late scholastics, or Spanish natural law
school.[16] Their intellectual project was to synthesize Thomistic philosophy and Roman Law. As I and others have shown, many of their conclusions were then borrowed and disseminated throughout Europe by the
jurists of the northern natural law school founded by Hugo Grotius and
Samuel Puffendorf in the 17th century.[17] Paradoxically, many of these
conclusions lived on into the 18th century, and even into the 19th, after
the Aristotelian and Thomistic principles that originally inspired them
had fallen from favor.

The core idea on which the theory was based was Aristotle's description of contract as voluntary commutative justice. In the *Nicomachean
Ethics*, Aristotle explained that while distributive justice secured for each
citizen a fair share of whatever wealth and honor the society had to divide, commutative justice preserved the share that each had received.[18]
Therefore, according to Aristotle, each party to an exchange had to give
something equal in value to what he had received.[19] Thomas agreed, and
used this idea to analyze the different ways in which an exchange could
be unfair.

For Thomas and Aristotle, then, and later for the scholastics and the
members of the northern natural law school, contract was defined in
terms of commutative justice: it was a voluntary exchange of things
equivalent in value. That approach troubled 19th century jurists, because

---

15. Cf. Gordley, *Philosophical Origins*, pp. 10-23.

16. Cf. *ibid.*, pp. 69-111.

17. Cf. *ibid.*; Hans Thieme, "Qu'cest-ce que nous, les juristes, devons à la seconde scolastique espagnole" in *La seconda scolastica nella formazione del diritto privato moderno*,
ed. P. Grossi (Milan, 1973), p. 7; Robert Feenstra, "L'Influence de la scolastique espagnole
sur Grotius en droit privé," *La seconda scolastica*, p. 377; Malte Diesselhorst, *Die Lehre
des Hugo Grotius vom Versprechen* (Cologne, 1959).

18. *Nicomachean Ethics* V ii.

19. *Ibid.*, V iv-v.

it seemed to involve mystical conceptions of economic value. Prices aren't fair or unfair; they are set by impersonal forces of supply and demand.

That objection did not trouble most people before the 19th century and, in my opinion, it should not trouble us. For Thomas, the late scholastics and the natural lawyers, the fair price of goods was the market price at the time of sale. They understood perfectly well that this market price had to fluctuate to reflect factors that they called need, scarcity and cost, which correspond closely to what we today call supply and demand.[20] Normally or eventually, they thought, the seller who charged the market price would recover his costs. Therefore, normally or eventually an exchange at the market price does not make either party richer at the other's expense. In that sense, it is a fair price. Often, they knew, prices will fluctuate, and the seller will recover more or less than his costs. But that situation had to be tolerated. In their view, prices had to fluctuate because they had to reflect not only cost, but need and scarcity. They seem to have regarded the market price as the fairest price practicable.[21] Moreover, they realized that exchange at the market price is fair in the same way a bet can be fair: the party who wins if prices change the next day could just as easily have lost. As Domingo de Soto, a jurist and theologian, observed in the 16th century: "as the business of buying and selling is subject to fortuitous events of many kinds, merchants ought to bear risks at their own expense and, on the other hand, they may await good fortune."[22]

I have argued elsewhere that this theory makes sense of the relief which our courts now give when a price is so high or low as to be "unconscionable."[23] Nearly always, the person who gets relief paid more or took less than the market price. In some cases, he agreed to such a price because, like a shipwrecked sailor in need of rescue, he was physically cut off from normal markets. In some cases, he agreed out of ignorance. For

---

20. Cf. Thomas Aquinas, *In decem libros ethicorum expositio*, ed. A. Pirotta (Turin, 1934), lib. 5, lec. 9; Thomas Aquinas, *Summa theologiae*, Biblioteca de autores cristianos, 3rd ed. (Madrid, 1963) IIa IIae q. 77, a. 3 ad 4; Leonardus Lessius, *De iustitia et iure, ceterique virtutibus cardinalis liber quattor* (Paris, 1628), lib. 2, cap. 21, dub. 4; Ludovicus Molina, *De iustitia et iure tractatus* (Venice, 1613), disp. 348; Hugo Grotius, *De iure belli ac pacis libri tres*, ed. B. J. A. de Kanter and van Ketting Tromp (Leiden, 1939) II xii, 14; Samuel Puffendorf, *De iure naturae et gentium libri octo* (Amsterdam, 1688), V i, 6.

21. Cf. Gordley, *Philosophical Origins*, pp. 98-101.

22. Soto, *De iustitia et iure*, lib. 6, q. 2, a. 3.

23. James Gordley, "Equality in Exchange," *California Law Review* 69 (1981), p. 1587.

example, a New York court gave relief to a man who had bought a refrigerator from a door-to-door salesman for three times the retail price he
would have paid in a nearby store.[24] In contrast, our courts would not
give relief, and we ourselves would have little sympathy, if a person complained he had been cheated on the price of his house because six months
after he bought it, housing prices fell, so that he lost money buying when
he did. He could just as easily have won. Moreover, there is no way to
eliminate the risk he ran without freezing housing prices, and we know
that if we did so, we would face the evils that economists describe: stocks
of unsold housing or queues of buyers.

It seems to me, then, that this older theory explains our intuitions and
those of our courts about when a price is fair. Moreover, far from con-
tradicting a modern economic understanding of prices, the theory can actually be sharpened by the insights of modern economics. We can see
more clearly today how, in a long-run stable equilibrium, the seller would
recover his costs, and what evils would ensue if we tried to eliminate price
fluctuations by freezing prices.

Having defined contract in terms of commutative justice, Thomas, and
then the late scholastics and natural lawyers, used the principle of equality to explain the obligations that the parties undertook implicitly when
they contracted. For Thomas, an action was defined by its end.[25] Knowing the definition, one could see what characteristics the action should
have. Thus, Thomas's starting point when he discussed the injustices that
are committed in buying and selling was his definition of sale: it is an act
of commutative justice in which money is exchanged for goods.[26] Therefore, a party could not sell defective goods for the price of goods that are
not defective.[27] Thomas thus showed why, because of its very definition,
a sale should be governed by the rule of Roman law that the seller of defective goods is liable to the buyer.

The late scholastics and the northern natural lawyers agreed. Some of
them explained that in particular circumstances, the parties might find it

---

24. Jones v. Star Credit Corp., 298 N.Y.S. 2d 264 (Sup. Ct. 1969). Cf. also Frostifresh v.
Reynoso, 274 N.Y.S. 2d 757 (Supr. Ct. 1967), *rev'd as to damages*, 281 N.Y.S. 2d 964 (App.
1967) (relief given when refrigerator that had cost the seller $300 sold for $900 plus $250
credit charges); American Home Improvement Co. v. MacIver, 201 A.2d 886 (N.H. 1964)
(relief given to party who agreed to pay $1750 plus $800 in credit charges for purchase and
installation of fourteen windows, a door and coating for sidewalls of his house).

25. *Summa theolgiae* Ia IIae q. 18, aa. 5, 7.

26. *Ibid.*, IIa IIae q. 61, a. 3.

27. *Ibid.*, IIa IIae q. 77, aa. 2-3.

advantageous to modify the terms that the law would otherwise read into their contract. They could do so, but not in a way that would violate equity. Thus Luis de Molina, a late scholastic, and Jean Domat, a 17th century natural lawyer and an admirer of Thomas, explained that the parties could agree that the seller will not be liable for defects. But they could do so only if the seller reduced the price to preserve equality.[28]

The sale of defective goods is one of the injustices we set out to explain. The older theory gives a reason why it might be unfair to sell a dilapidated house on a cesspool to unsuspecting immigrants: they might be paying the price of a flawless house and receiving a defective one. If so, commutative justice is violated because exchange requires equality. Similarly, the wages of the workers might not reflect their risk of injury on the job or their lack of job security.

It would seem, however, that by this older theory any of these contracts might be fair if the price or wages did reflect the defects or the risks. To decide whether this theory explains what is truly unjust in the situations Sinclair described, we have to consider why the contract price might or might not reflect all the risks.

If we make two assumptions, we can conclude that no one would ever make a contract that violates commutative justice by placing a risk on a party who is not fairly compensated for bearing it. One assumption is that all parties are fully aware of the risks that a contract imposes on them. Another assumption is that as long as a party receives the amount necessary to induce him to bear a risk, he is fairly compensated. If a buyer or an employee would pay $10 to be rid of a risk, a seller or employer who wishes him to assume it must offer at least a $10 reduction in the price or a $10 increase in his wages. A seller or employer would make the offer only if he could not bear the risk himself more cheaply. It might be he could eliminate the risk by some preventative measure that cost $8. Or it might be that he would be willing to bear the risk for $8 for the same reason that an insurance company can better bear a risk than its customers. It can better bear the risk of fire than a homeowner because it runs the risk over and over and can set off the extra money it makes when it wins against its losses when it loses. If, for either reason, the seller or employee were willing to bear the risk for $8, he would never transfer the risk to someone who would only bear it for $10. One can see this conclusion easily by thinking of the reduction of risk as one would

---

28. Molina, *De iustitia et iure*, disp. 353; Jean Domat, *Les Loix civiles dans leur ordre naturel* (Paris, 1713), 30 i. iv. 2.

think of any improvement in a product: anyone who can make it for $8 and sell it for $10 will do so. That is so independent of any assumptions about the bargaining power of consumers or employees or the competitiveness of the market.

Accordingly, a contract can violate commutative justice as these earlier authors understood it, only if these assumptions do not hold. Consequently, if in a particular case we are convinced that a contract did not fairly compensate a party for a risk it imposed on him, it must be that these assumptions do not hold. Either the disadvantaged party did not fully understand the risks he assumed, or the amount he would pay to avoid assuming a risk is not really fair compensation.

One possibility is that a party did not understand the risks he assumed. He was willing to bear a risk for an extra $2, but—if he fully understood it—he would only bear it for $10.

A second possibility is that the party fully understood the risk and was paid the amount necessary to induce him to bear it, but nevertheless the amount he was paid still is not fair compensation. This possibility does not arise in the world of the modern economist. Economists concern themselves with efficiency, not fairness. Moreover, for an economist, efficiency is a matter of satisfying preferences backed by cash. Given a certain distribution of wealth, a result is more efficient if one person can be made better off without making anyone worse off. Whether he is better off, however, is determined by what he will pay. If Upton Sinclair's workers can be induced to walk unfenced catwalks over boiling tubs of meat for an additional nickel, the result is efficient, and there is no standard by which one can say it is unfair.

In the world of Thomas Aquinas and Aristotle, however, it is perfectly possible that a person who is undercompensated for bearing a risk might choose to bear it anyway. It could happen in two ways. First, the worker might not be prudent. Second, the worker might be the victim of distributive injustice.

Prudence, for Aristotle and Thomas, is right reason about things to be done. Through prudence, we choose what is good[29] and weigh the importance of good and evil consequences.[30] In the world of Aristotle and Thomas, then, choices are not merely preferences backed by cash. It is possible to choose rightly or wrongly, to choose what is good or what is

---

29. *Nicomachean Ethics* VI v; *Summa theologiae* IIa IIae q. 47.
30. Thomas Aquinas, *De veritate*, q. 5, a. 4 ad 4, in Thomas Aquinas, *Opera omnia*, ed. P. Ficcadori (Parma, 1859).

bad for oneself. If a worker runs some terrible risk for slight compensation, we can at least entertain the possibility that the worker is imprudent, and that his employer is exploiting his imprudence to undercompensate him.

Or it may be that the worker is the victim of distributive injustice. He is so poor that it becomes prudent for him to take appalling risks because his other alternatives are worse. Many of the episodes Sinclair described are of this kind. Old Antanas risks his life working in a cold, unheated cellar, and Jurgis risks his death inhaling fertilizer, because their alternative is to let their families starve. An economist would have to say the result is efficient. The economist can only talk about efficiency given the initial distribution of wealth. The distribution itself is neither efficient nor inefficient. In the Aristotelian and Thomistic tradition, however, the distribution can be unfair.

In this tradition, then, contract is commutative justice and requires equality. Equality is violated when a person is undercompensated for the risks the contract places upon him. He might be undercompensated because he does not fully understand the risks. Or he might be undercompensated because his imprudence has been exploited or because the distribution of wealth itself is unjust. The older theory, then, can address a question that the more modern theories of contract do not: Why and when is a contract unfair?

Moreover, I also think that this older theory best explains the law that now governs the problems Sinclair described. While I cannot give a detailed description of the law here, a short sketch will be enough to show why I think so.

One problem was liability for defects in objects sold. At the time Sinclair wrote, American courts were in the process of scrapping the rule *caveat emptor* and borrowing from continental Europe the Roman rule that the seller implicitly warrants his goods against defects.[31] Initially, if the seller did not want to warrant his goods, he could disclaim liability for defects in the contract. Later, the courts began holding that under some circumstance such a disclaimer was "unconscionable" and therefore void. The leading case was *Henningsen v. Bloomfield Motors*.[32] A man had bought his wife a new Buick. She was injured because the

---

31. Cf. William Prosser, "The Implied Warranty of Merchantable Quality," *Minnesota Law Review* 27 (1943), p. 117 at pp. 130-136.

32. 161 A.2d 69 (1960)

brakes were defective. Buick had inserted a clause in the contract limiting liability to the cost of replacement and repair. The court held that Buick could not disclaim liability for physical injuries. Today, when goods are new and a defect causes physical harm, virtually all courts hold the manufacturer liable whatever the contract says, although he is now said, in lawyers' language, to be strictly liable in tort rather than liable on an implicit warranty that cannot be disclaimed in contract.[33]

As a matter of commutative justice, this result makes sense. Of course, the manufacturer could reduce the price of factory new goods sufficiently to compensate the buyer fairly for the risk of physical injury. But the manufacturer would be unwilling to do so if he himself could bear the risk more cheaply. He alone knows what it would cost to prevent defects by spending more on quality control. Even if a defect cannot be prevented, the risk that it will injure someone physically is present to roughly the same degree and with roughly the same potential for harm, whenever he sells a car. It is a risk he encounters repeatedly, and therefore a risk he, like an insurance company, should be better able to bear than a person who faces it only once. If, indeed, he can bear this risk the most cheaply, then it is hard to believe that he compensated the buyer fairly for assuming it. Most likely, the buyer did not understand the legal consequences of the disclaimer or the likelihood of a defect as well as did the seller. The court in *Henningsen* noted how unlikely it was that the buyer understood what the seller was disclaiming.

Courts have been more willing to allow the seller of used property to disclaim liability for defects.[34] They have been more willing to allow a seller to disclaim liability for commercial harm caused by a defect.[35] These are precisely the cases in which it is less clear that the seller, if anyone, could prevent the defect and that the risk is the same for every product he sells. With used goods, defects are less preventable, and dealers often handle heterogeneous merchandise that creates different risks for different buyers. When damage is commercial, the amount of harm that a defect will cause varies with the buyer's use of the goods, as do the pre-

---

33. Cf. W. Page Keeton, Dan B. Dobbs, Robert E. Keeton and David G. Owen, *Prosser and Keeton on the Law of Torts*, 5th ed. (St. Paul, Minnesota, 1984); Richard A. Epstein, *Cases and Materials on Torts*, 6th ed. (Boston, 1995), pp. 861-862.

34. *E.g.*, Crandall v. Larkin, 334 N.W.2d 31 (S.D. 1983); Tillman v. Vance Equipment Co., 596 P.2d 1299 (Or. 1979).

35. Cf. Uniform Commercial Code § 2-719.

cautions the buyer himself might take to prevent the damage. It is less certain that the seller can more cheaply bear the risk, and therefore more likely the buyer was fairly compensated for doing so.

The second problem is liability for injuries on the job. Four years after *The Jungle* was published, New York enacted the first workers' compensation statute.[36] All states now have such laws.[37] They hold the employer liable even absent fault for all injuries arising out of his employment. The rationale often given is that otherwise, "the burden will fall upon the worker who [is] least able to support it."[38] Indeed, the employer's burden normally will be smaller for the reason already described: the employer, like an insurance company, faces it repeatedly and single workers do not. We can see, then, why the employer should be liable as a matter of commutative justice. If the employer can bear the risk at lower cost, he cannot be increasing the wages of his employees enough to compensate them fairly for bearing it. It is unfortunate that it took legislation to hold the employer liable. Courts should have held him liable simply as a matter of contract law.

We can also see why the employee's recovery should not be barred on the ground that he assumed the risks of his employment or that he was negligent himself. The workers' compensation statutes typically abolish these defenses.[39] Absent such a statute, supposedly, an employer can still rely upon them if he is sued for negligently failing to provide a safe workplace.[40] Nevertheless, courts have found ingenious reasons for allowing the employee full recovery. Some courts have held that the employee can recover when the employer violated a safety statute because otherwise the beneficial purpose of the statute might be frustrated.[41] The California Supreme Court has required the employer to prove that the accident wouldn't have occurred if the employee had been careful, and then made this proof difficult.[42]

The last problem is that of job security. Here the law is changing and its final shape is unclear. The traditional rule is that, unless otherwise agreed, a contract of employment is terminable at will by either party for

---

36. 1910 N. Y. Laws 625.
37. *Prosser and Keeton on Torts*, p. 573.
38. *Ibid.*, p. 572.
39. *Ibid.*, p. 573.
40. *Ibid.*, p. 575.
41. *E.g.*, Koenig v. Patrick Construction Corp., 83 N.E.2d 133 (N.Y. 1948).
42. Gyerman v. United States Lines Co., 498 P.2d 1043 (Cal. 1972).

any reason or no reason. Courts have been uncomfortable with the rule. The result has been a steady enlargement of employees' rights to job security, accompanied by great confusion.

In a majority of states, courts are willing to treat descriptions of company policy contained, for example, in employee handbooks as promises incorporated in the employment contract. If the handbook describes a procedure for firing employees or says that no one will be discharged except for cause, the employer has to follow the handbook. To avoid that result, employers have sometimes said in the handbook, for example, "This handbook is not a contract and contains no promises" and the management "can cancel all personnel policies with or without notice." Often, courts have not been sympathetic. In one case, the language I have just quoted was held not to be binding, not only because it was insufficiently conspicuous, but because it was ambiguous.[43] Absent an express provision in a handbook, moreover, some courts have been willing to infer a promise from the employer's practices in the past.

The Supreme Court of Michigan thought it had to go even further to protect job security. In *Toussaint v. Blue Cross and Blue Shield*,[44] the court rested the employees' rights, not on contract, but on what it called "a situation instinct with an obligation." The employer had created this situation by establishing personnel policies that secured "an orderly, cooperative and loyal workforce" by giving "the employee the peace of mind associated with job security and the conviction that he will be treated fairly."[45] Therefore, the employer was liable. This opinion attracted considerable attention among legal scholars because, while all of us had heard of liability based on contract, none of us had previously heard of liability based on a situation instinct with obligation.

The problem seems to be that while the courts are expanding the rights of employees, they are still clinging to a 19th century view of where contractual obligations come from. Therefore, they strain to find something to call a promise, and when they can't, they stop talking about liability based on contract. The approach we are recommending better explains what they are actually doing. The question ought to be whether it is more onerous for an employer to respect a particular right or for the employee

43. Sanchez v. Life Care Centers of America, Inc., 855 P.2d 1256 (Wyo. 1993). Other courts, however, are quite willing to give effect to such disclaimers: *e.g.*, Johnson v. Morton Thiokol, Inc., 818 P.2d 997 (Utah 1991).

44. 292 N.W.2d 880, 892 (Mich. 1980).

45. 292 N.W.2d at 892.

to do without it. If the burden of firing an employee only after a hearing or only for cause is less onerous for the employer than the burden of termination at will for the employee, it would be odd indeed if the employer had really increased his employees' salaries sufficiently to compensate them for bearing it. It is more likely that the employees do not realize the extent to which they are exposed to the risk of being fired arbitrarily. In such a case, as a matter of commutative justice, the employer should not be allowed to discharge at will.

Most of the cases involving employment handbooks and established practices are of this kind. The handbook or practice is evidence that protecting a right is less onerous for the employer. It is also evidence that the employees are not being compensated fairly for running a risk of which they are probably unaware. Nevertheless, it is only one source of evidence. In an appropriate case, when the contract is silent and the court is convinced that the terminability at will is a greater burden for the employee, it should hold that the contract is not terminable at will. In an extreme case, it could hold that for the employer to reserve a right to terminate at will is unconscionable.

Rights to job security are a remaining patch of the social and economic jungle that Upton Sinclair described. Clearing it will be easier if we can see our way more clearly through the intellectual jungle which the 19th century lawyers left behind them.

Equity *Contra* Inequality:
A Response to James Gordley

Edwin M. Epstein

It is a pleasure to participate in this exchange with Jim Gordley, a colleague and friend of many years' standing, particularly in light of the challenging argument he has offered.

It is noteworthy that two papers in this colloquium, *Labor, Solidarity and the Common Good,* deal with the concepts of property and contract. These legal constructs are the institutional cornerstones of the socio-economic system of production, distribution and exchange, characterized by continuous and ubiquitous transactions, we call "market capitalism." Indeed, they go to the heart of what Karl Polanyi, in his classic work on the evolution of western market society, called "the great transformation."[1]

Professor Gordley's paper brings to mind the insights of another eminent scholar, Wolfgang Friedmann, who emphasized, in *Law in a Changing Society*, that equality — that is, between contracting parties — and freedom of will — that is, each party's unhampered ability to make meaningful choices — are elements crucial to the formation of contractual relationships. Friedmann's insistence on equality and freedom of will ties in very closely, I suggest, with the emphasis Professor Gordley's paper lays on commutative justice. Accordingly, I wish to begin my comments by quoting Friedmann:

> The social function of contract in the formative era of modern industrial and capitalist society may be summed up in four elements: freedom of movement; insurance against calculated economic risks; freedom of will; and equality between the parties.[2]

Friedmann observes that the initial stages of market capitalism's emergence, extending roughly from the 16th through the 18th centuries, were marked by an effort to realize these ideals fully and comprehensively. One must say "ideals" because, as the illustrations Professor Gordley draws

---

1. Karl Polanyi, *The Great Transformation* (Boston: Beacon Press, 1957).
2. Wolfgang Friedmann, *Law in a Changing Society* (Baltimore: Penguin Books, 1964), p. 89.

from Upton Sinclair's *The Jungle* remind us, dramatic disparities developed between capitalism in concept and capitalism in reality—often enough, in grim reality, enforced by contract—during the 19th and early 20th centuries.

Reflecting upon Professor Gordley's discussion of Aquinas's notion of commutative justice, with its emphasis on equality, I am struck by a certain complementarity Aquinas's notion bears to Friedmann's four foundational elements. I shall focus especially on the elements of equality and freedom of will, and suggest why the courts—particularly during the last fifty years—have sought to develop some clear notions of justice/fairness in contractual relationships, consistent with these latter two, underlying norms.

What are the essential elements of justice/fairness with respect to contracts? We need only look to the structure of contemporary industrial/post-industrial market society to appreciate why the courts have imputed (and legislatures have incorporated) into contractual relations prohibitions against, or limitations upon, particularly unconscionable, one-sided agreements: viz., agreements in which one of the parties lacks a meaningful choice concerning key elements of the transaction—so-called "contracts of adhesion." The category includes, *e.g.*, contracts providing for usurious interest rates, patently onerous terms and conditions of employment, or requirements that the purchaser of a consumer item must secure (and pay for) further, unwanted services or financing from the seller.[3] Judicial and legislative interventions against such contracts reject the legitimacy of commercial relationships which depend upon decisive inequalities or asymmetries in the parties' bargaining positions, which undermine one party's freedom to exercise meaningful choice, and which—consequently—abrogate justice-as-fairness and, indeed, fundamental human dignity.

Inequality in contractual relationships can take many forms. For example, unequal access to pertinent information erodes the capacity of a contracting party to exercise the virtue of prudence, or the capacity to act in light of a full consideration of alternative courses of action. In our modern, highly industrialized, highly technological society, the ability of a contracting party (and here, I have in mind the individual consumer) to act prudently is much more tenuous than at an earlier time, when buyer and seller were party to greater common knowledge, to fuller "symmetry of information," concerning the nature of a good—say, a horse or an

---

3. For a classic discussion of this topic, cf. Friedrich Kessler, "Contracts of Adhesion—Some Thoughts About Freedom of Contract," *Columbia Law Review* 43 (1943), pp. 629ff.

agricultural implement—or of a service—say, transportation of products by wagon or boat—than present-day commerce typically allows.

What do most of us *really* know about the underlying attributes or precise character of the goods and services we buy? What do you know, for instance, about the terms and conditions of the health insurance contract you have purchased—a contract which has (and this pertains to freedom of will), in all probability, been offered to you on what amounts to a "take-it-or-leave-it" basis, rather than through a process of information-sharing and negotiation? By way of illustration, here at Saint Mary's College employees may choose between two health insurance providers, Kaiser Permanente or Foundation Health (albeit, with HMO and PPO options). With regard to what these providers' packages actually specify—their costs, terms of access to and availability of services; indeed, what services, in reality, they provide—one party to the contract, the insurer-provider, is far more fully informed than the other, the individual Saint Mary's faculty/staff member. The individual purchaser is not —and, as a practical matter, cannot be—a party to the negotiations which establish the contract's detailed terms. Moreover, the insurer-provider defines the terms of the relationship, a relationship thus rendered asymmetrical so far as the information-base and bargaining positions of the parties are concerned. Even officials of the College who negotiate these agreements enjoy, by comparison to the provider, limited information and bargaining leverage. The essential point here is that the contracting parties hardly meet as equals, and that individual and institutional consumers exercise very limited freedom of will, under these conditions.

Asymmetry between contracting parties' knowledge or information naturally suggests another point regarding Friedmann's four elements of contract, a point which bears, again, on equality between the parties and their freedom of will. I refer to the issue of power, and of power's impact upon the bargaining positions of parties to a contract.

Consider the packing-house laborers of *The Jungle*, who toiled over boiling vats of meat, under exceedingly hazardous conditions: What, truly, was their realm of choice—their sphere of discretion—concerning the terms and conditions of their work? They had a job offered to them... if they were "fortunate" ... which they could take or leave. The grinding poverty under which they lived was such that the alternative—not to work—was merely a formal, empty alternative. In short, their freedom of will—the condition they brought to the work contract—was severely constrained in another sense. Although they were the employer's "peers" in information about the horrible work conditions, they remained nearly powerless to act otherwise than as a consequence of their reduced circumstances. So also with the first of Friedmann's elements, freedom of movement. Though nominally "free to leave," these workers were in no position to go anywhere: alternative forms of employment were, very often, non-existent—or equally as unattractive and dangerous as working in the slaughterhouse. As a practical matter, contracting to work in the Jungle captured by Sinclair's prose hardly amounted to the exercise of real choice; frequently, there was no meaningful alternative.

Thus, we are led once again to the heart of the question: absent parity in bargaining position or leverage, and absent viable alternatives, did individuals—do individuals—have the effective capacity to pursue their interests prudently, *viz.*, by contract? Inequality in bargaining power, lack of meaningful—practicable—choice, constrained mobility: these extra-contractual factors gave to one party, the meat-packing companies, an asymmetrical bargaining position in the marketplace, to the detriment of the other party, the individual worker.

The essential, countervailing value that attaches to Aquinas's—and, before him, to Aristotle's—concept of commutative justice is, of course, *equity*. I am not employing the term in the technical, legal sense which goes to the distinction between the common law, evolved in the Law Courts, and the system of equity, as developed in the Chancery Courts. Rather, I am invoking equity in the "lay" or "common"-sense which goes to what the courts, particularly during the post-World War II era, have sought to enforce by way of promoting justice-as-fairness in contractual relationships. It is, I suggest, the ever-growing complexity of the market system that has stimulated courts to emphasize the norm of equity. The more complex the market, the more readily it generates antecedent asymmetries between parties to contracts. Judges have sought to restore equity —justice-as-fairness—to contractual relationships shaped by a market system whose very complexity has rendered its basic, original, governing assumptions—Friedmann's four, elemental principles—largely inoperative.

I am, then, in fundamental agreement with Professor Gordley: a more explicit understanding, on the courts' part, of the requirements of commutative justice might have saved our legal system from undertaking dubious, conceptual "leaps" and "stretches" in the interest of restoring equity, broadly conceived, to contractual relationships which have been shaped by exigent inequalities. Still, although legal reasoning has, indeed, been stretched—perhaps, strained—on occasion, such judicial "creativity" has, arguably, also proved essential to the on-going quest for a dynamic, flexible market system—equitable as well as efficient, ethical as well as enterprising.

3

Aquinas's Account of the Ineradicably Social Character of Private Property

Thomas A. Cavanaugh

In this paper, I present what, for the moment, I will call Aquinas's account of private property. I hesitate so to name his account, for, it will become evident that Aquinas offers a conception of private property that differs significantly from current usage. For example, Aquinas maintains that a needy person has a claim in justice to the abundance others possess. He holds that a needy person who takes from the abundance of another in order to satisfy his own urgent, manifest, unmet need does not steal, for he takes what belongs to him insofar as the goods of the earth are ordained to satisfying human need generally.[1] Thus, Thomas understands private property to have an ineradicable social dimension. In what follows, we will, first, briefly survey both the standard contemporary account of the private ownership of goods and that account's justificatory difficulty; second, present Aquinas's account; and, third, conclude with a number of practical reflections.

I

The Standard Contemporary Account

In a recent survey of private property's conceptual topography, Jeremy Waldron notes:

> The person to whom a given object is assigned by the principles of private property...has control over the object: it is for her to decide what should be done with it. In exercising this authority, she is not

---

1. Cf. *Summa Theologiae* IIa IIae, q. 66, a. 7; also IIa IIae q. 33, a. 7 ad 3.

understood to be acting as an agent or official of the society. Instead, we say that the resource is *her property*; it *belongs* to her; she is its *owner*; it is as much *hers* as her arms and legs, kidneys and corneas.... [H]er right to decide as she pleases applies whether or not others are affected by her decision.[2]

Further analyzing the standard conceptualization of private property, Waldron states:

[A]n individual's right to make decisions about the use of a thing has two elements. First... it implies the absence of any obligation to use or refrain from using the object in any particular way. The owner may decide as she pleases and she is at liberty to put her decision into effect by occupying, using, modifying, perhaps even consuming or destroying the object. Second, private property implies that other people do not have this liberty; they *do* have an obligation—an obligation to the owner—to refrain from occupying, using, modifying, consuming or destroying the object.[3]

Waldron finds that private property is to be conceived as an obligation-less exclusion of others from the enjoyment of what is one's own that incorporates others' obligations to leave alone one's own things, which are taken to be comparable to one's organs.

II

The Problem of Justification

This account, however, faces a significant, normative, justificatory difficulty. Indeed, those who propose the conception Waldron outlines are acutely aware of the difficulty of justifying private property so conceived. Waldron articulates the problem:

[W]e look for a justification of private property, because it deprives the community of control over resources which may be important

---

2. Jeremy Waldron, "Property Law" in Dennis Patterson, ed. *A Companion to Philosophy of Law and Legal Theory* (Cambridge: Blackwell Publishers, 1996), p. 6 (emphasis original).

3. *Ibid.*, p. 7 (emphasis original).

to the well-being of its members, and because it characteristically requires us to throw social force behind the exclusion of many members of our society from each and every use of the resources they need in order to live.... [R]esources may gradually come to be distributed in a way that leaves a few with a lot, a lot with a very little, and a considerable number with nothing at all. Private property involves a pledge by society that it will continue to use its moral and physical authority to uphold the rights of owners, even against those who have no employment, no food to eat, no home to go to, no land to stand on from which they are not at any time liable to be evicted.[4]

Clearly, if one has an abundance of life's necessities and others are in dire need of them, one's exclusion of them from what they need in order to survive requires significant justification. Yet, in terms of what standard could one justify such a social institution? If one were to attempt to justify private property so conceived in terms of the greater good of the greater number, one would—at least, on the face of things—fall short of facing the specific problem noted by Waldron. For the point of that problem is that massive quantities of property—and of its most significant manifestation, capital—tend to be concentrated in the hands of a very small minority.[5] One might resort to the claim of efficiency, *viz.*, that this concentration of property in the hands of a few actually increases the welfare of all. Yet, such a claim must fail to meet the demand on two counts. First, it is asserted that some lack what they need in order to survive (and, certainly, some do lack these basic resources, while many more lack what they need in order to flourish). How is private property of benefit to them? Second, there is no reason to think that efficiency could not be just as readily served by amassing great quantities of property in the hands of a few non-owning managers, as do publicly traded corporations and large pension and mutual funds.

Trying another tack, one might justify excluding those in dire need from the use of what others possess in abundance by asserting that those who do not have what they need in order to survive are no worse off simply because others have more than what they need in order to survive and

---

4. Waldron, *op. cit.*, p. 9.

5. As Waldron notes, John Locke, who faced this difficulty, thought the convention of money both allowed some to accumulate significantly more than others and justified their accumulation, for he understood money to express a society's acquiescence in the fact of some having much more than others.

flourish.[6] Yet, this response also misses the justificatory demand, for the problem is: Why ought those who do not have what they need in order to survive refrain from taking from the abundance of others? The most realistic answer asserts what is no doubt usually true: Those who do not have what they direly need are in no position to threaten the superabundance of others. This response, however, asserts might; it does not make might right.

III

The Root of the Problem: Conceptual Dualism

If those in dire need are excluded from what others possess in abundance, private property is not readily justified. Indeed, one suspects that in facing this justificatory problem, what one in fact faces is the more deep-seated problem of conceptual dualism that plagues much of contemporary Anglophone philosophy. To see this, we need merely revisit the path to the problem of justification. First, others were conceptually excluded from the enjoyment of things they need and, under threat of coercion, required to honor their own exclusion; second, a justification for this coerced exclusion was sought, but none was forthcoming. The final resolution of this problem will be to discover that private property is a contingent, but ineliminable fact of our existence, or the only viable way of handling property, or the way that most recently won out. These responses, however, manifest the hallmark of most problems generated by conceptual dichotomies: they leave the intellect dissatisfied by asserting that the way things are just is, inexplicably, the way things are.

Take, for example, the conceptual dichotomy of dichotomies, the mind-body problem. To generate the mind-body problem, define the mind and body as utterly distinct and independent of one another; second, note that the mind and body have a close, intimate, inimitable association with one another, to the point that the mind exerts occult, causal influences over the body, and *vice-versa*. Third, note that this salient association of mind and body is conceptually inexplicable, leading one—perhaps—to deny the existence of mind, or driving one to assert haplessly that this relationship just is, serendipitously, the way things are.

---

6. Economists classically refer to this sort of emendation as a "Pareto improvement."

Or—for a derivative, less celebrated instance of conceptual dichotomy —take billiard balls and other efficient causes as the only type of causality; next, noting that reasons certainly do seem to be causes for human action, define human action as the spatio-temporal movement of body-parts. Now you are in position to ask, pointedly: How can a reason, a mental entity, cause a local motion? Not being a billiard ball, or even billiard ball-like, a reason cannot be a billiard ball-like cause of an action.[7] Therefore, reasons cannot be causes, though every sane person treats them as if they were.

The point, one hopes, has not disappeared into the convolutions of these examples. Insoluble philosophical problems often depend on faulty conceptions that divide what obviously belong together: soul and body, motive and action... bread and the satisfaction of human hunger.

The specific point, bearing on the exclusionary conception of private property, is that such a conception, by needlessly introducing a dichotomy between what one possesses and others' claims to that which they urgently need, generates the unsatisfiable demand that one justify some having a tremendous amount of the goods of this earth, while others lack what they need in order to survive. How could one justify sustaining one man's possession of a full granary in the face of one starving human being, let alone in the face of a starving village? One cannot. Any supposed justification would either have to deny the problem or show itself to be morally bankrupt.

IV

Aquinas's Account

Setting aside the exclusionary account, let us investigate the conception of private property proposed by Aquinas: namely, the conception that property is possessed privately, yet is at root always ordered towards common use, or the "private possession/common use" account of property.

At the outset, let us note that Aquinas follows and develops Aristotle's account, and the positions of—amongst others—Ss. Ambrose and Basil. Moreover, Catholic social teaching, as found in such documents as Leo

---

7. For an account which makes reasons serendipitous occasions of motion, cf. Davidson, "Actions, Reasons, Causes" in *Essays on Actions and Events* (Oxford: Clarendon Press, 1980).

XIII's *Rerum novarum* (ns. 111-113), Pius XI's *Quadragesimo anno* (n. 191), John XXIII's *Mater et Magistra* (ns. 428-429), Paul VI's *Populorum Progressio* (ns. 22-24), and John Paul II's *Centesimus annus* (Chp. IV), consistently employs this private possession/common use (or universal destination) account of private property.

Following Aristotle (*e.g., Politics B* v, 1263a40), Thomas distinguishes the possession of property from the use of property. He offers three allied reasons for the social institution by which private individuals possess and control property, that is, by which they acquire, hold and distribute goods.[8] First, he notes what has come to be called the "Tragedy of the Commons" argument: where people hold things commonly, the common lot suffers; on the other hand, where each has his own, individuals are more solicitous for what they can call "mine."[9] Thomas asks us to imagine a house with many servants in which the common work goes undone (a memory, perhaps, of his boyhood at Rocca Secca); or, we might reflect on the "family" garden going unweeded, or envision the myriad papers scattered in the entrances of non-owner occupied triplexes. Second, Thomas notes that, the narrowness of fallen human self-interest notwithstanding, where things are not assigned to individuals, there arises a practically inefficient disorder and confusion concerning precisely who should care for exactly what. Finally, he offers what one might call the "good fences make good neighbors" argument: private property makes for a more pacific commonweal, for each can be contented with what he can, with clarity, call his own.

In short, Thomas understands private property to be a natural, practically intelligent way of holding goods. He does not—as many thinkers do—preoccupy himself with the criterion of initial distribution, with how property is first assigned to individuals, *e.g.,* whether by discovery, occupation or work. This is not to say that he, or the tradition of which he is a part, is indifferent to the question of how we determine who gets what. The latter question is, however, relatively moot in Aquinas's account. For, regardless of how we decide to assign property to the possession of private individuals, the issue of the use and point of property is ineradicably rooted in natures, and this brings us to the heart of Thomas's account: the goal-oriented character of goods, and of our possession of goods.

8. *Summa Theologiae* IIa IIae q. 66, a. 2.
9. For the same argument, cf. Waldron, *op. cit.,* p. 11.

V

The Ends of Things

With respect to the use of property, Thomas holds that while property ought to be held individually, it is always by its very nature ordered primarily towards a common use—namely, towards meeting the needs of human nature—regardless of who possesses it. Thomas offers reasons for this conclusion from sacred theology as well as from secular philosophy. Let us attend to the philosophical grounds. In answering the question whether it is licit for men to possess things,[10] Thomas refers to an earlier question concerning the killing of plants and animals.[11] In that earlier question, he argues that because we are higher beings than plants and animals, we may kill and eat plants and animals; moreover, because animals are higher beings than plants, we may kill plants and feed them to animals.

Thomas understands humans to have the abilities to domesticate, dominate and kill and eat plants and animals, because our nature is higher than those of plants and animals and because plants and animals are ordered towards sustaining human life. Thus, to be counted among its excellences is a plant's or an animal's edibility by humans. There are, of course, innumerable other ends, or excellences, of edible things: to sustain themselves in being, to pollinate flowers, to make soil, to fly, to swim or to display beauty (as Gerard Manley Hopkins sings:

> As Kingfishers catch fire, dragonflies dráw fláme
> ....
> Each mortal thing does one thing and the same...
> Selves—goes itself; *myself* it speaks and spells,
> Crying, *Whát I dó is me: for that I came*).[12]

Even as food living things serve ends beyond the mere sustenance of human life, *e.g.*, the ends of human flourishing, conviviality and sociability. In Aquinas's account of property possession, the basic end of human survival and the higher ends of human flourishing are connected. For now, however, let us focus on the basic end of human survival, since

---

10. *Summa Theologiae* IIa IIae q. 66, a. 1.
11. *Ibid.*, q. 64, a. 1.
12. Gerard Manley Hopkins, *Poems and Prose* (New York: Penguin Books , 1987), p. 51.

it indicates, most radically, the point and justification of consuming things, one of the more profound instances of the use of a thing.

Can one argue that plants and animals are *ordered* towards sustaining human life, and not merely *capable* of sustaining human life? Most of us unreflectively eat what is put before us; we do not bother to justify our eating, and thereby indirectly killing, peas and carrots or chickens and pigs. If we were to offer a justification for our eating these other living beings, we might rely solely on our ability to do so. In accordance with such a justification, being "higher" on the food chain would simply mean being able to kill and eat other beings that are, lacking such a power over humans, "lower" on the chain. Yet, given such a justification, what would be wrong with an animal's killing and eating a human being? Or why ought we not kill and eat other humans?

Taking the issue of cannibalism, it is—fortunately—not normally necessary, and it would usually be a great inconvenience, to kill and eat other human beings. Moreover, being human beings, we might generally oppose the killing and eating of humans, at the very least out of enlightened self-interest. Such responses, however, would have us hold that killing and eating other humans is merely ill-advised, inconvenient, disagreeable or generally unnecessary. It is not, surely, for such reasons that we *ought not* to kill and eat other human beings. We ought not to do so because they are beings of reason and will, who apprehend and direct themselves towards the enjoyment of what is good. It is for this very reason that we may kill and eat animals and plants: while we do, they do not, apprehend the good, nor direct themselves towards it. We humans are higher, more perfect, better beings than plants and animals. Thus, when we kill and eat plants and animals, plants and animals achieve a better level of existence by serving higher, human ends. The carrot and the rabbit fuel thought, and thereby participate in a level of existence far surpassing that of a root or a rodent; the crushed grape serves human sociability, and thereby rises above its own limits. When lower beings serve our needs, they become more perfect, and realize a level of being far above that of their entire species.

On the other hand, if a human were eaten by, *e.g.*, a Bengal tiger, this order would be reversed. Indeed, even if Bengal tigers would become extinct unless one tiger should happen to eat a human being, nevertheless, human flesh which supports thought and will would thereby be reduced to sensation and perception, at best. The more perfect would have been subordinated to the less perfect, and that ought not to be.

Thus, Thomas justifies the most profound use of things, consumption, in terms of the hierarchical relationship between the natures of things and human nature. To the extent to which a justification for eating plants and animals rises above the superficial claim that it is "okay" to eat them... because we can, that justification will tend towards the hierarchy-of-natures account that Thomas offers. In terms of such an account, one can indeed argue that plants and animals are ordered towards sustaining human life, and that it is therefore not merely possible, but proper to make use of them.

At the outset of this paper, I noted that Thomas holds that were a man's basic needs to go unmet in a manifest way, such that others in possession of an abundance of the earth's goods did not voluntarily give him what he needed, he could take—not steal—from their abundance what he needed in order to survive, for this would belong to him. This position follows from Thomas's justification of that profound and total form of use, eating. By justifying the consumption of things in terms of the hierarchical relation between human and non-human natures, Aquinas grounds his claim that urgent, unmet, manifest need makes goods common. For possession, inasmuch as it is a means to use, does not eradicate the order of natures upon which use is based. Moreover, possession itself clearly *is* a means to use. It is perverse to have simply to have, and we recognize this by wanting to have for the sake of something better than having, namely, for the sake of using. Thus, insofar as use is grounded in human nature's need, and possession is ordered toward use, human need always "trumps" possession; the just limits of one man's abundance are to be defined by his neighbor's needs.

Of course, just as food is not solely for nutrition, so possession is not solely for meeting basic needs: it also enables us to flourish, and this brings us to a consideration of the role of virtue, its relation to the use of possessions in Thomas's account. Earlier, we spoke of things serving basic human needs and ends, and of things serving higher human ends, or more generally, of things serving human flourishing. In Aquinas's account, virtues transform one man's basic human need into another man's opportunity to achieve perfection, or to flourish through the exercise of virtues such as justice and generosity.

The virtues of distributive justice and generosity at once depend upon goods being possessed privately and serve as the stimuli by which deeds make use common. For Thomas, following Aristotle, understands that individuals control property in part for the sake of having something to share and to give to others. Were property not under the control of private individuals, the purview of the virtues of distributive justice and generosity would be unduly constrained, for few avenues would be open to the private individual to exercise these human perfections and, thereby, to flourish as a human being. Moreover, for Aquinas's account of common use to bear fruit in the relief of those who lack property, the human perfections of generosity, magnaminity and justice must be realized in the deeds of those who possess property in abundance. Aristotle himself alludes to this when he says:

> [I]t is better for possessions to be privately owned, but to make them common property in use; and to train the citizens to this is the special task of the legislator.[13]

The private possession/common use account of property avoids the justificatory problem which morally disables exclusionary accounts of private property. In so doing, it emerges as a truly political account. For, it depends upon a community of citizens who, possessing abundance, understand themselves to be perfected by their speedy and voluntary distribution of that abundance to those in need; hence, it must face the truly profound difficulty of making citizens good. Indeed, one further reason Thomas offers in justification for the private individual's possession of goods is so that he may speedily and *easily* [or "readily" — *facile*] communicate them to others in need.[14]

VI

Concluding Observations

Let us conclude on what may be called a practical-theoretical note, or — if you will — with a reflection on the practicability of theory. What must be done in order to realize something like the private possession/common use account of property in practice? It is tempting to think in terms of institutions, of tax schemes, social welfare programs or tithing. Such temptations ought to be resisted, however, at least as initial answers. For, what we need most is reconceptualization, not programs or processes. The latter will inevitably follow from a renewed understand-

---

13. Aristotle *Politics B* v, 1263a40.
14. *Summa Theologiae* IIa IIae q. 66, a. 2.

ing of what we, as human beings, are and of what it means for us to be better human beings.

We must reapprehend ourselves as the highest-natured beings in a world of natured beings. With respect to other human beings, we must come to know and to think of ourselves as genetically social creatures, naturally from, with and for others: beings who regard themselves as, *of course*, given to watching out for their fellows; who think of themselves as, *of course*, dedicated to wide and deep social goals. No tax scheme can do this for us. Neither can any institution realize Aquinas's account while hampered, as present institutions are, by a pervasive, adversarial, "autonomous-man" view of humanity, an account which claims that human solidarity, human society, is no more than an artifice whereby we over-top a nature "red in tooth and claw in ravine."

The task, then, is two-fold: first, to clean our contemporary conceptual stables of the detritus that has come to litter them; second, to present an account of human nature that keeps together what must be kept together: the one and the many, the strong and the weak.

The Spirit of Poverty:
A Response to Thomas Cavanaugh

Wayne H. Harter

Professor Cavanaugh begins his discussion, "Aquinas's Account of the Ineradicable Social Character of Private Property" with reference to an article from the *Summa Theologiae*[1] on theft. He does this in order to bring out how very different is St. Thomas's understanding of private property from the understanding now current. Indeed, the claim, "... whatever certain people have in superabundance is due, by natural law, to the purpose of succoring the poor,"[2] is worlds apart from the (contemporary) position that private property

> ...implies the absence of any obligation to use or refrain from using the object in any particular way. The owner may decide as she pleases and she is at liberty to put her decision into effect by occupying, using, modifying, perhaps even consuming or destroying the object.[3]

With Cavanaugh, then, one hesitates even to use the term "private property" when speaking of Aquinas's teaching, given the confusion liable to be caused in the minds of contemporary listeners.

In case it is not yet plain just how radically different Aquinas's notion of property is from modern notions, let me recall a few remarks he made in connection with the article on theft, before taking up the main burden of this response. The third objector to an article asking "Whether it is lawful for a man to possess a thing as his own?"[4] answers in the negative, quoting St. Ambrose, "Let no man call his own that which is common property." St. Thomas responds to this objection by supplying a neglected distinction between ownership and use—invoking the principle which is at the heart of Professor Cavanaugh's paper—and thereby de-

---

1. St. Thomas Aquinas, *Summa Theologiae* IIa IIae q. 66, a. 7.

2. *Ibid.*

3. Jeremy Waldron, "Property Law," in *A Companion to Philosophy of Law and Legal Theory*, cited above, p. 64.

4. *Summa Theologiae* IIa IIae q. 66, a. 2.

fends the right of the individual to possession of property. However, Thomas qualifies his defense of private possession with a further quotation from St. Ambrose, *viz.*, "He who spends too much is a robber." Now, it would be a mistake to interpret the phrase "spends too much" as a simple condemnation of lavish expenditure, for St. Thomas understands *magnificence* to be a virtue.[5] Rather, "spends too much" seems to be an indictment of those who spend beyond life's necessities before meeting the needs of the poor. In any event, what is interesting in this connection is that in the mind of St. Thomas it is not the poor who are guilty of misdeed, but rather the wealthy, when the former are in the position of having to appropriate the goods of the latter.

This conclusion is confirmed in the article immediately following, concerning the essence of theft, wherein St. Thomas refutes an objector who, relying again on the authority of St. Ambrose, asserts: It is no less a crime to take from him that has, than to refuse to succor the needy when you can and are well off.[6] This objector goes on to conclude: therefore, just as theft consists in taking another's thing, so does it consist in keeping it back. To understand Aquinas's somewhat indirect response to this argument, we must keep in mind that the precise question under scrutiny is whether or not secrecy is something that completes the definition of theft; in this light, the objector's equation of "taking" with "keeping back" is simply not to the point. Thus, St. Thomas does not argue that the two acts are incomparable. Quite to the contrary: having delineated the three elements which define theft (contrary to justice, concerning things possessed, and committed in secrecy), St. Thomas writes, "To keep back what is due to another inflicts the same kind of injury as taking a thing unjustly: wherefore an unjust detention is included in an unjust taking." When the poor are forced—even put in the position of needing—to appropriate the superabundance of goods in the hands of the rich, a sin of withholding property unjustly—equivalent to theft or robbery—has already taken place. If, then, it were necessary to underscore the radical character of St. Thomas's understanding of the rightful possession of property, we could add: were one to ask St. Thomas, "Should the thief be punished, when one who is desperately poor is forced to take from one who is rich?" he would, no doubt, answer that the thief should be punished—and St. Thomas would likely add, in suffering punishment

---

5. *Ibid.*, q. 134.
6. *Summa Theologiae* IIa IIae q. 66, a. 3. o. 2.

the wealthy one will avoid putting in further danger his eternal salvation.[7]

Moving now to the main argument of my response to Professor Cavanaugh's paper, we must note Professor Cavanaugh's warning that his paper attends solely to the philosophical grounds of St. Thomas's discussion. This restriction sets aside those theological principles which, by adding their own dynamic to the problems of property, would complicate the argument. Still, the occasion of these reflections is the inauguration of the John F. Henning Institute, dedicated to Catholic social thought, and the conjunctum of faith and reason suggested by the Institute's mission demands that we offer some account of how an adequate social doctrine must proceed under the light of faith. A Christian philosophy — or so I would argue — while it ought never to confuse distinct orders of inquiry, nevertheless can attain the fullness of wisdom, its proper end, only in relation to the theological truth which forever exceeds merely philosophical competence.[8]

What I wish to suggest is this: St. Thomas's discussion of the possession of property, taken in light of the fullness of his teaching, calls us Christians — and especially those of us who, in modern parlance, are owners of capital — beyond even the legitimacy of private property.[9] Thereafter, I wish to point out one, concrete means of heeding St. Thomas's call.

The theological principle to be invoked here is the perfection of nature by grace. Professor Cavanaugh speaks to a cardinal tenet of Catholic social teaching when he argues for private ownership/common use of property. But as evidenced by recent papal encyclicals, the counsels of Christian perfection, animated by the spirit of charity, direct us at this point in our history toward a more perfect relationship to wealth. We must there-

---

7. Cf. *ibid.*, q. 62, a. 2: Whether restitution of what has been taken away is necessary for salvation?

8. I have in mind the argument of Jacques Maritain in *An Essay on Christian Philosophy*.

9. "No one, certainly, is obliged to assist others out of what is required for his own necessary use or for that of his family, or to give to others what he himself needs to maintain his station in life becomingly and decently: 'No one is obliged to live unbecomingly.' But when the demands of necessity and propriety have been met, it is a duty to give to the poor out of what remains. 'Give that which remains as alms.' These are not duties of justice, except in cases of extreme need, but of Christian charity, which obviously cannot be enforced by legal action" (Pope Leo XIII, *Rerum novarum*, n. 36).

fore begin by asking what relation the institution of private property has to the natural law.

In the first article to *Summa Theologiae* IIa IIae, Question 66, St. Thomas affirms that it is natural for man to possess external things. As Professor Cavanaugh has, quite rightly, pointed out, Thomas's conclusion follows from man's relative superiority in being over things. Yet, because the question turns upon the hierarchy of species — kinds of beings — this right to possession is established only in regard to man as such; no principle of the natural law concerning the actual distribution of wealth among individual men can be deduced from the superiority of mankind to things. It is, therefore, in the second article to Question 66, concerned with the legality of *a* man possessing a thing as his own, that St. Thomas attempts to address what we call private property. We should keep in mind that the form of the question, "Whether it is lawful for a man to possess a thing as his own?" suggests that a proper understanding of the natural law would incline one to answer, "No."[10]

If we take the definition of law in general, "an ordinance of reason for the common good, made by him who has care of the community, and promulgated,"[11] then it is obvious why the institution of private property, *as private*, is no part of the natural law. Of course, *as ordained to the common good* — or common, social use — private property can be made to *partake* of law. This is why Aquinas argues *both* that what the natural law actually prescribes is the common use of all goods, *and* that how these goods are divided or distributed in order to achieve the common good is not itself dictated by natural law, but is a matter for human law.[12] Whether property is possessed by individuals or in common is a matter to be decided by the prudent legislator, according to the exigencies of history, *i.e.*, of his time and place.

We can see evidence of Aquinas's own recourse to history in at least two, the first and third, of the justifications he gives for the private possession of property. The second justification, the argument to good order, is different in that not only does it appear to be applicable to all times and places (it recalls St. Thomas's discussion of the necessity for order,

---

10. I am indebted to James Murphy for the rhetorical significance of the article's form.

11. *Summa Theologiae* Ia IIae q. 90, a. 4.

12. *Summa Theologiae* IIa IIae q. 66, a. 2 ad 1.: "Because the division of possessions is not according to the natural law, but rather arose from human agreement which belongs to positive law... [H]ence the ownership of possessions is not contrary to the natural law, but an addition thereto devised by human reason."

even in the state of unfallen nature, wherein some still would rule over others[13]), but also in that, while it certainly supports the institution of private property, it does not appear to be essentially tied to it. On the other hand, the first and third justifications, the arguments from universal selfishness and the threat of civil strife—arguments Professor Cavanaugh refers to as "the Tragedy of the Commons" and "good fences make good neighbors"—are significantly different arguments; that is, they are not reducible to the problem of order, except so far as one is engaged in a justification of private property. Within another ordering of goods, they would not of themselves add considerations beyond those which are covered by the need for order. We shall have more to say on this point. For the moment, we should also note that the two justifications' rational character devolves from the accidental condition of human nature, *i.e.*, from the limitation of human goodness owing to Original Sin.

The question, then, naturally arises: Does the institution of private property—an application of justice to the exigencies of fallen nature—exhaust the possibilities for a rational distribution of goods destined to common use? Is private property merely one possible way among others for ordering well the natural community of goods? Furthermore, if there exist other ways, is private property the *best* way? Any answer to the last question must, of course, recognize that various historical circumstances may elicit a variety of "best" practices. All the same, given that the two reasons essential to justifying private property devolve from human failing, one would suspect that "Yes" to the first question would suggest "No" to the second. If private property must be understood as an accommodation to weakness, it seems that the Christian must work to overcome reliance upon it in the course of the journey toward sanctity.

There is no doubt that St. Thomas himself knew of a distribution of property based otherwise than upon private ownership, and even embraced it as the higher way.[14] As a religious living the cenobitic life, St. Thomas was intimately familiar with a distribution of goods that repudiated individual ownership. From their very foundations, Christian religious communities uniformly embraced the practice of voluntary poverty. As we see in the *Institutes* of John Cassian, the great organizer of Western monasticism, there was little need even to explain the importance of poverty to the way of perfection:

---

13. *Summa Theologiae* Ia IIae q. 90, a. 4.
14. Cf. *Summa Theologiae* IIa IIae q. 186, a. 3.

Among their other practices I find that it is unnecessary even to mention this virtue, *viz.*, that no one is allowed to possess a box or basket as his special property, nor any such thing which he could keep as his own and secure with his own seal, as we are well aware that they are in all respects stripped so bare that they have nothing whatever except their shirt, cloak, shoes, sheepskin, and a rush mat; for in other monasteries as well, where some indulgence and relaxation is granted, we see that this rule is still most strictly kept, so that no one ventures to say even in word that anything is his own: and it is a great offense if there drops from the mouth of a monk such as an expression as "my book," "my tablets," "my pen," "my cloak," or "my shoes"; and for this he would have to make satisfaction by a proper penance, if by accident some such expression escaped his lips through thoughtlessness or ignorance.[15]

No doubt, within monastic life human weakness issuing in selfishness and eliciting strife posed serious threats to the integrity of the community. The extensive lists of punishments suitable to a variety of offenses are proof enough that monastic communities remained thoroughly human communities. Nonetheless, the religious orders succeeded (and still succeed) in creating communities wherein great numbers found (and find) the highest fulfillment of their humanity; so, there is evidence that the dangers can be overcome, necessities procured, charity prevail. This brings us back to the second justification for private property, the appeal to order.

A rational ordering of persons to things can be attained, as it was in the monastery, just as easily through a relation defined by stewardship as through one defined by ownership. Certain monks were charged with certain things, like the cooking and eating utensils, for the sake of their care and conservation. These goods delegated to the care of the monk were, in a sense, "his," at least so far as their good condition reflected, and largely depended upon, his labor. The monk could see himself in his work, could view the things entrusted to his care as instruments of his own perfection and as the means whereby he personally contributed to the good of the community. Thus, the human inclinations toward selfishness and strife were curbed, at least, through the institution of stewardship. We should now ask after the significance of this monastic prac-

---

15. John Cassian, *Of the Institutes of the Renunciants,* trans. Rev. Edgar C. S. Gibson in *The Nicene and Post-Nicene Fathers* vol. XI (Oxford: James Parker and Co., 1894), IV. XIII.

tice for our own communities. Before proceeding to the question, however, a few observations are in order.

The rejection of private property follows from the monk's quest for a
holiness that exceeds any ethic establishable under law. It is a counsel of
Christian perfection. For that reason, we must admit that the sort of community in property practiced by the monasteries is not simply *another*
way in which the distribution of wealth can participate in the natural
law; it is a way made possible only through the supererogation of charity. For the same reason, we must realize that the life of common possession is one that cannot be legislated for secularized societies. The law-
giver who attempted the abolition of private property for the sake of
universal perfection would be suffering a mistaken sense of order and
committing an injustice. All this is true. Yet, while the counsels of perfection are above the natural law, we would fall into grave error should
that fact tempt us to conclude that the counsel of poverty or the institution of communal property need not inform our political aspirations. The
gifts and fruits of the Spirit are above the law, and because they are above
the law they are capable of perfecting it.

As St. Thomas reminds us, no one who has not professed vows can be
bound by a counsel of perfection; but even though one is not bound by
the counsels, one falls into sin if one despises them.[16] In the encyclical letter of Pope Paul VI, *Populorum progressio*, "turning toward the spirit of
poverty"[17] is listed as a condition for human development. But what does
Paul VI mean?

In its most obvious sense, "poverty" refers to the lack of external
things necessary to a fully human existence. Considered in itself, therefore, poverty is an objective evil. To be deprived of that which is necessary to our natural end is to be obstructed in our development toward
happiness. Nevertheless, because our final end transcends this world, and
is even imperiled by undue attachment to wealth, voluntary poverty can
become a means of purification. "Man," writes St. Thomas,

> is directed to future happiness by charity, and since voluntary
> poverty is an efficient exercise for the attaining of perfect charity, it
> follows that it is of great avail in acquiring the happiness of
> heaven.[18]

---

16. *Summa Theologiae* IIa IIae q. 86, a. 3.
17. *Populorum progressio*, n. 21.
18. *Summa Theologiae* IIa IIae q. 186, a. 3 ad 4.

The *spirit of poverty*, I suggest, refers to the embracing of this counsel to the degree allowable by our duties and station in life.[19] As lay Catholics, we are not bound — more, we are not permitted — to undertake the radical poverty of a Father Charles de Foucauld, who left the Trappist monastery in order more perfectly to follow the humility and poverty of Christ.[20] However, we are bound to see in his act a more perfect, more perspicuous manifestation of our own way to sanctity. In this light, the spirit of poverty means the determination to possess no more than is necessary for virtue; it means a radical detachment from the things of the world; and while our particular duties may require great wealth indeed, the spirit of poverty means a readiness to divest ourselves of any superabundance for the sake of God and neighbor.

The spirit of poverty, then, suggests that superabundance is a good only so far as it is an opportunity for sacrifice. In the *Summa Theologiae*, St. Thomas puts the challenge to what we are calling the spirit of poverty in the most compelling terms, religious terms. He entertains the following argument. Man's ultimate perfection lies in happiness, and riches are the means to happiness: therefore, poverty is not required for religious perfection, as is suggested by the Scripture, *Blessed is the rich man who is found without blemish*, and supported by philosophy when it recognizes, *Riches contribute instrumentally to happiness*. St. Thomas replies:

> It is not said simply that the *rich man* is blessed, but *the rich that is found without blemish, and that hath not gone after gold*, and this because he has done a difficult thing, wherefore the text continues (verse 9): *Who is he? and we will praise him; for he hath done wonderful things in his life*, namely by not loving riches, though placed in the midst of them.[21]

This teaching on the spirit of poverty has (if one may be permitted to speak this way) even more relevance for us than for those living in the time of St. Thomas. The consistent theme of the social encyclicals, since the publication of *Rerum novarum*, is the extraordinary condition of the modern world, marked — among other things — by an unconscionable disparity in wealth. A privileged few enjoy unprecedented riches, while

---

19. *Ibid.*, ad. 6: The renunciation of one's wealth is compared to almsgiving as the universal to the particular, and as the holocaust to the sacrifice.

20. Pope Paul VI pays tribute to this "Universal Brother" at *Populorum progressio*, n. 12.

21. Cf. *Summa Theologiae* IIa IIae q. 186, a. 3 ad. 4 and res. 4.

many others—even the majority—are without the necessities of a fully human life, some starving and without shelter. The Church, therefore, persists in calling upon all persons of goodwill to overcome the situation. The actual means of so doing—on a global scale, and with sufficient stability—belong to the competence of economists and political leaders, guided by an adequate philosophy of man, but the Church has suggested, among others, one particular way toward the socialization of property that holds immense, largely untapped, promise.

When Leo XIII addressed the plight of non-owning workers, he did so through the demand for a just wage and the appeal for almsgiving. A just wage was understood to be one "sufficiently large to enable [the worker] to provide comfortably for himself, his wife and his children," and if he "gladly practices thrift," to allow him to "come into possession of a little wealth."[22] Forty years later, while reaffirming Pope Leo's teaching on the just wage, Pope Pius XI nevertheless added:

> We consider it more advisable in the present condition of human society that, so far as possible, the work-contract be somewhat modified by a partnership-contract.... Workers and other employees thus become sharers in ownership or management or participate in some fashion in the profits received.[23]

This call for a genuine sharing in the ownership and management of production has been repeated by subsequent popes,[24] perhaps most eloquently by John Paul II, who says, "...on the basis of his work each person is fully entitled to consider himself a part-owner of the great work bench at which he is working with everyone else."[25]

This shift from the mere insistence on a just wage, toward a social understanding of property, appears to be the result of a deepening understanding of the subjectivity of work. As expressed by Paul VI:

> Economics and technology have no meaning except from man whom they serve. And man is truly only man in as far as, master of his own acts and judge of their worth, he is author of his own advancement, in keeping with the nature that was given to him by his

---

22. *Rerum novarum*, n. 65.
23. *Quadragesimo anno*, n. 65.
24. Cf. Pope John XXIII, *Mater et magistra*, nn. 77, 92; *Gaudium et spes*, n. 68; Pope John Paul II, *Laborem exercens*, n. 14.
25. *Laborem exercens*, n. 14.

Creator and whose possibilities and exigencies he himself freely assumes.[26]

It is, therefore, understandable that Leo XIII limited the call to charity, in *Rerum novarum*, to the question of almsgiving, and that we now should understand charity to be leading us to enable, so far as possible, all men and women to become co-owners of the means necessary to their development into fully human persons.

Socialization of the means of work is, perhaps, the most obvious place from which to begin the task. But it would not do to overlook the further possibilities suggested here. With one such, I am personally familiar. I myself own an undivided share in a 14,000+ acre horse ranch. With other owners, I am able to provide my family with recreational opportunities otherwise beyond the reach of a typical academic's means. Various sorts of stewardship have been established for the maintenance of this large enterprise, and on a more occasional basis, opportunities abound for owners to contribute freely to the common good by fence-mending, stable repair, and so on. The important thing, the thing to be stressed, is that the sense of ownership does not come at the cost of community, nor the sense of community at the cost of a sense of responsibility for the property: selfishness and strife are continually overcome. Who can say what advances for the dignity of man could be achieved if, with a little imagination, the same principle of common ownership were applied, even elevated, in the context of freely-formed Catholic communities, founded for the preservation and fulfillment of spiritual and family life? Certainly, we stand before a future rich in possibilities.

Recognizing the distinction between that which we hold in trust and that which we hold at discretion, we, as lay Catholics engaged in the Apostolic work, must seek to ennoble the lives of those in want. Given that the act of charity proceeds above the law, it belongs to the spirit of poverty to guide and make luminous our secular undertakings. Let us, then, take to heart the warning and exhortation of Pope Paul VI, writing in what is surely one of the most remarkable documents of the twentieth century:

> We want to be clearly understood: the present situation must be faced with courage and the injustices linked with it must be fought and overcome. Development demands bold transformations, innovations that go deep. Urgent reforms should be undertaken without

---

26. *Populorum progressio*, n. 34.

delay. It is for each one to take his share in them with generosity, particularly those whose education, position and opportunities afford them wide scope for action. May they show an example, and give of their own possessions as several of Our brothers in the episcopacy have done. In so doing, they will live up to men's expectations and be faithful to the Spirit of God, since it is "the ferment of the Gospel which has aroused and continues to arouse in man's heart the irresistible requirements of his dignity.[27]

---

27. *Populorum progressio*, n. 32.

4

Managers as Distributors of Justice: An Analysis of Just Wages in the Tradition of Catholic Social Thought[1]

Michael Naughton

Our incomes are like our shoes;
if too small, they gall and pinch us;
but if too large, they cause us to
stumble and trip.

Charles C. Colton,
English clergyman (1822)

In 1995, compensation for the CEO of Green Tree Financial, Lawrence Coss, totaled $65.5 million; during the same period, a credit manager for the same company, Rob Albin, received $21,000, and worked a second job to make ends meet: the shoes, it may be said, did not fit.[2] Colton's metaphor captures an enduring truth about pay: a good fit between employees' pay and their humanity is an important, organizational condition both for human development and for development of an effective,

1. I am indebted for helpful critiques or suggestions to Stuart Herman, Robert Wahlstedt, Robert Kennedy, Ernest Pierucci, Jim Grubbs, Mick Sheppeck, Colleen Striegel, and my students at the University of Saint Thomas. I am especially grateful for S. A. Cortright's editorial skill, which has strengthened the argument of this paper.
2. Scott Carlson, "Done with Disparity," *St. Paul Pioneer Press* (April 6, 1995), pp. 1E-2E; for an analysis of the sources and effects of gross disparity in executive vs. employee compensation, cf. Douglas M. Cowherd and David I. Levine, "Product Quality and Pay Equity Between Lower-level Employees and Top Management: An Investigation of Distributive Justice Theory," *Administrative Science Quarterly* (June 2, 1992), pp. 302-320. On the explosion in dual and triple job-holding in the wake of wage stagnation and decline (a burden which falls with surprising disproportion upon women), cf. Richard B. Freeman, ed., *Working Under Different Rules* (New York, 1994).

working community among the members of an organization. When large numbers of employees witness their pay stagnate or decline, we see rampant galling and pinching; when executives are paid exorbitant salaries and bonusès, we sense personal stumbling and tripping; and when both galling and stumbling mark the same organization, disillusion, cynicism and hostility abound.

This is not to argue that Coss and Albin should be paid the same; it is to note that in determining pay, as in most human activities, we can err by either excess or defect: we can pay too little or too much. Just as shoes must fit the physical dimensions of the human foot, must be neither too small nor too large, so systems of compensation must fit the moral dimensions of the human organization, paying neither too little nor too much. The employee who doubts "Am I paid fairly?"[3] never responds with a relativistic shrug. Because nothing bears more directly than pay upon everyone's standard and quality of living, dubious compensation incites even the most radical relativist to the rhetoric of justice. Just as there are no atheists in foxholes, so there are no relativists when just compensation is in question.

Historically, the standard for determining wages has been a "moral standard."[4] In the Old Testament, Jeremiah condemns those who cheat workers of their wages: "Woe to him...[W]ho works his neighbor with-

---

3. Compensation works a formative effect on both those who provide it and those who receive it, as well as on society at large. The "hot" issue of executive compensation should be analyzed not only in light of how it affects the bottom line or of what the market will bear, but also in light of how it affects the fit between an organization's mission and practice, of how it affects all employees (including executives), and of how it affects the good order of society. Both for those who determine it and for those who receive it, compensation is a signal opportunity to practice the virtue of justice or its opposed vices—graspingness, niggardliness, and so on—both so as to become what they practice and to shape the character of the institutions which support their practices. It is, then, a matter of urgent concern for everyone whether those charged to determine compensation ask the human, *telos* questions which bear on the promotion of human virtue: What kinds of practice, fitted to what kind of person, am I promoting? what kind of organization, fitted to support such persons and practices, am I promoting? what kind of society could welcome such an organization?

To restrict discussion of compensation to market forces is to neglect the fundamental human questions: Who are we? what kind of economic community ought we to fashion? It fails to address the fundamental truth that the quality of our deeds shapes the quality of our persons. Viewing compensation *solely* or *merely* as an expression of impersonal market forces neglects the role of compensation in the formation of human character, at peril both to the immediate organization and to the wider community.

4. John A. Ryan, *The Living Wage* (New York: The Macmillan Company, 1906), p. 40.

out pay, and gives him no wages" (Jer. 22:13). The New Testament relaxes Jeremiah's standard not at all: St. James prophesies,

> Here crying aloud are the wages you withheld from the farm hands who harvested your fields. The shouts of the harvesters have reached the ears of the Lord of hosts... (Ja. 5:4-5)

and the Lord's "justice will not sleep forever." So, too, in Islam, the worker must be justly compensated before "his sweat dries."[5] Recently, John Paul II declared that a family wage verifies "the justice of the whole socioeconomic system," as an irreplaceable litmus-test of its integrity.[6]

The Judeo-Christian tradition has long highlighted the moral dimension of wage-paying, asking: Are managers and employers *distributors of justice?* do employees receive what they need? do they earn what they contribute? can employers compete at the same time as they pay just wages? Unfortunately, this tradition of evaluating wages by the standard of justice is largely missing from contemporary theory and practice.[7] The theory and practice of human resource management treat pay primarily in strategic terms: *the purpose of pay is to attract, reward, retain and motivate employees who best achieve the strategic goals of the organization.* These strategic goals tend to be exclusively economic in nature: beating the competition, growing market share, enhancing quality, raising customer satisfaction and retention, increasing efficiency, motivating performance, maximizing shareholder wealth.

From the strategic point of view, compensation is an instrument for increasing the economic value of the organization. If paying executives

---

5. S. A. Ali, *Social and Economic Aspects of the Islam of Mohammed* (Lewiston, Maine: The Edwin Mellen Press, 1993), p. 103.

6. John Paul II, *Laborem Exercens: On Human Work* (1981), n. 19.1, in Michael Walsh and Brian Davies, eds., *Proclaiming Justice and Peace* (Mystic, Connecticut: Twenty-Third Publications, 1984), pp. 271-311. Even in secular literature, wages never escaped the pale of justice, although the bases of justice were disputed. Ricardo reduced just wages to market wages; Marx reduced the market wage to an unjust device for capitalists' appropriation of surplus value added to manufactures by labor. Even today, discussion of rising executive pay versus the stagnation of most wages occurs under the horizon of the question, Is it just? For the Catholic Church's position on just wages, 1891-1958, cf. Jean Yves Calvez and Jacques Perrin, *The Church and Social Justice* (Chicago: Henry Regnery Company, 1961), pp. 239-245.

7. The Hay Group, leaders in compensation consulting who owe their foundation to a devout Quaker, offer a distinct counter-example; cf. Thomas P. Flannery, David A. Hofrichter and Paul E. Platten, *People, Performance and Pay* (New York: The Free Press, 1996), p. xv.

100-200 times the wage of the lowest-paid employee, or paying sub-living wages, or reducing health benefits and pensions, promotes the organization's economic goals, then it is strategically justified. By the same token, if paying executives no more than five times the wage of the lowest-paid employee, or paying above-market wages, or increasing employees' benefits, promotes the organization's economic goals, then its makes equal strategic sense. Speaking purely strategically, if employees are to be treated justly, that treatment owes nothing to their inherent, personal dignity; rather, they are to be treated justly because justice happens to make strategic sense. Justice, then, becomes one strategic option to enhance the organization's strategic position. As a mere "means," justice can always be among many, which may or may not be useful, depending upon whether it can "trumped" by an appeal to strategic advantage.

A defense of the inherent justice of "strategic compensation" is forthcoming only if the value of the employee's labor is exhausted by the pay determined under strategic goals. The strategic view is dominated by "objective dimensions" of work: that is, by how pay affects profits, productivity and the quality of products; by what motivates employees to add economic value; by what techniques — e.g., market-based comparisons, gainsharing, profit sharing, stock options — can secure and advance the organization's economic goals. Many of these "objective" determinants of pay are, in fact, critical to a just system of compensation. Nevertheless, so far as the strategic mind tends to admit only objective and quantitative factors, and to reduce compensation to a technical calculation, it fails to respect the *whole* reality of work for pay.

Strategic systems of compensation neglect the *subjective dimension* of work. Work is not simply an activity that find its *terminus ad quem* — or, lands out — in a product. As a reflexive activity, work "lands" right back in the person, the working human subject. This subjective dimension of work should persuade us that human work can neither be understood nor regulated through strategic goals alone, however important those goals are. Every person must ask, "What is work doing *to* me, as well as *for* me, and *for* others?" In its very nature, work is, for the worker, a self-transforming — inherently moral and spiritual — activity. Indeed, *because* work is other-transforming, it transforms the worker.[8] Failure to account

---

8. As James Murphy puts it, "...action is immanent (that is, perfects the self) only because it is transitive (perfects the world); self and world are jointly articulated in the act of labor" ("A Natural Law of Human Labor," *The American Journal of Jurisprudence*, 1994, pp. 71-95).

for the subjective dimension of work precipitates a collapse into a kind of "economism," that is, into an ideological commitment to a materialistic view of the organization, driven exclusively by attention to the objective dimensions of work.

Integrating work's objective and subjective dimensions is one of the greatest challenges posed to modern managers. If they look to reform organizations without due regard to the objective dimensions of work, chaos will reign as the prelude to bankruptcy. If they look to reform organizations without due regard to the subjective dimension of work, a different — but no less destructive — chaos will reign: namely, moral and spiritual stagnation.[9]

An exclusive focus on the demands of the organization's economic objectives, as these implicate pay, crowds out and marginalizes the subjective meaning of work and the subjective value of the organization itself.[10] Far more is at stake in the pay-relationship between employer and employee than whether strategic goals will be met. Due regard for the subjective dimension of work redirects discussion of human labor from the kind of work being done to "the fact that the one who is doing it is a person."[11] The ultimate *raison d'être* of pay is not strategic and objective, but developmental and subjective.

Attention to the subjective dimension of work tells us that pay is incommensurable with the work done; that is, pay can never truly compensate — never exhaust — the human act of labor. When people work, they leave — in the *form* of their products, but *in virtue of who they are* as images of the Creator — an irrepeatable imprint on the world which is, in its turn, an image of the creative activity of God. No price — no usable good, nothing exchangeable for goods — can stand as adequate recompense for this, the proximate source of all such goods. Hence, it is better to avoid speaking of pay primarily in terms of exchange, and to speak

---

9. Yet, exclusive focus on the objective dimension of work is simply a strategic bias, albeit one with deep roots in Western civilization. When it comes to work, the moral imaginations of thinkers otherwise as different as Aristotle and Frederick Taylor share a deep impoverishment, since it enters into neither to treat human labor except through its objective dimension. Like contemporary strategic thinkers, because these philosophers "had reductively explained the division of technical efficiency and human nature, they left no room for moral and social freedom" (James Murphy, *op. cit.*, pp. 17-18).

10. This habit of mind tends to be rooted in managers' university education, where a good portion of the curriculum is devoted to so-called value-added techniques of compensation, all of which aim to enhance profitability and production.

11. John Paul II, *Laborem exercens*, n. 6.

of pay instead as the expression or token of a work-relationship between employer and employee that is, at its core, a moral and spiritual relationship. The Judeo-Christian tradition insists that what is critical to the quality of this relationship is not *only* its "strategic" bearing, but also the "subjective dimension" through which work *works* to develop—for better or worse—each party to the relationship.[12]

This is precisely why the wage-relationship is best understood in terms of justice. To honor the subjective value of employees' work *via* their wages, managers must engage employees in right relationships, through the virtue of justice. Justice, from the Latin *ius*, means "right"; hence, the just person is in *right relation* to others or, in the words of Aquinas, is "well-disposed towards another."[13] Moreover, this right relation is a condition of one's own moral/spiritual—human—flourishing.[14] Compensation, then, is no mere exchange, but is a "side" of a relationship which should dispose employees rightly—justly—both to one another and to the firm. Catholic social thought over the past century has taught consistently that the manager, as a "distributor of justice,"[15] exercises the ability to put employees in right relationship with the organization by distributing wages that are *living, equitable* and *sustainable*.[16]

---

12. For a fuller treatment of this topic, cf. *Laborem exercens*, no. 6. The relation between work's subjective value and wages here presented is indebted to Josef Pieper's treatment of the *honorarium*, "An honorarium implies than an incommensurability exists between performance and recompense, and that the performance cannot 'really' be recompensed" (*Leisure, The Basis of Culture* (New York: Random House, Inc., 1963), p. 52ff.), to which Ernest Pierucci drew the author's attention. To recognize the incommensurability between labor and wage is to recognize the transcendent human dignity of the worker, and erects a barrier against the reduction of work to merely technical performance, suited to automata. Entrepreneurs and human resource managers honor themselves as well as their employees when they take employees' work seriously as a token of the dignity and mystery of human labor.

13. St. Thomas Aquinas, *Summa Theologiae* IIa IIae q. 58, a. 12.

14. Cf. *ibid.*, IIa IIae q. 57, a. 1. Within the Christian and classical traditions, justice ranks as the most excellent (and complete) of the cardinal virtues, precisely because it is other-related.

15. Or, as Clarence Walton named the manager, "dispenser of justice" (*The Moral Manager* (New York: Harper and Row, 1988), p. 218); cp. Aquinas, *op. cit.*, IIa IIae, q. 61, a. 1.

16. Employees stand to the larger human organization less as a part to a whole than as a whole to a whole. The virtue of justice binds the individual person and the organization in a right relation whereby the good of the individual is at the same time the good of the organization, a confluence of real, shared-but-undiminished [*sc.* in being distributed] advantages called "the common good"; cp. Aquinas, *op. cit.*, IIa IIae q. 58, a. 6. John Finnis notes, "...no common enterprise can itself bring about the all-round flourishing of any individual. An attempt, for the sake of the common good, to absorb the individual altogether into com-

Still, managers cannot be distributors of justice, nor can they rightly honor their employees, unless—in the words of Aquinas—their souls are "entirely possessed by justice," their intentions converted to the common good.[17] Eliot's Becket admonishes us against

> "…the greatest treason:
> to do the right deed for the wrong reason."[18]

Apart from the fundamental solidarity of right relationships with their organizational colleagues, employees shrivel into small-minded "strategic maximizers" in their own right, persuaded that their sole concern lies with their with own, narrow advantage, blind to the good of the organization as a whole and deaf to the promptings of the greater, common good.

* * *

It bears emphasis that, throughout this paper, the argument in no wise repudiates the strategic view of pay. On the contrary, the argument is indebted to the insights and programs generated by the strategic view. Under the influence of strategic theory, human resource management has developed effective wage-systems which bear study and emulation. "Right hearts" absent technically sound programs degenerate into sentimentality; to attempt a "moral" account of pay apart from due regard to strategic concerns is to court empty abstractions, frustration and, eventually, despair. Nevertheless, by failing to incorporate the subjective dimension of work and its implications, strategic wage-theory has missed the moral logic by which alone pay is intelligible in a fully human way. Accordingly, this paper essays one model through which (1) to take seriously the strategic insights of contemporary human resource management, and (2) to embed those insights in a properly human—i.e., moral and spiritual—understanding of work-relationships and work-communities.

---

mon enterprises would thus be disastrous for the common good, however much the common enterprises might prosper" (*Natural Law and Natural Rights* (Oxford: Clarendon Press, 1980), p. 168).

17. St. Thomas Aquinas, *Commentary on Aristotle's Nicomachean Ethics* (Notre Dame, Indiana: Dumb Ox Books, 1993), p. 302; cf. *Summae Theologiae* IIa IIae q.58, a. 3. In the Catholic tradition justice poses not only "What should I do?," but "Who should I become?"

18. *Murder in the Cathedral*, Part I, in *The Complete Poems and Plays, 1909-1950* (New York: Harcourt, Brace and World, 1952) p. 196.

Distribution of Pay and Right
Relationships: Forgotten Criteria

In the Judeo-Christian tradition, to ask whether a wage is just is to ask three essential questions: Is it a living wage (does it address human need)? Is it an equitable wage (does it honor the worker's contribution to the common enterprise)? Is it a sustainable wage (does it meet the demands of a viable economic order)? Answering "Yes" to these three questions is not as easy as first it may appear; a just wage is a complex and difficult achievement, entailing tremendous insight, sensitivity, competence and balance in the face of organizational and societal contingencies. Still, each affirmative answer constitutes a step in the direction of justice.

As the word itself suggests, managers are people who come of age, and help others to come of age. They can create organizational conditions suited to human development; they can foster the growth of employees into partners in the advancement of those conditions: they can, in short, act as agents of the common good. The organizational conditions essential to human development include: meeting employees' human needs — the principal vehicle, *a living wage*; eliciting employees' best contributions to the enterprise — the principal vehicle, *an equitable wage*; contributing to a viable economic order — the principal vehicle, *a sustainable wage*. To these three, vital elements we now turn.

1. A Living Wage

The Principle of Need.[19] When employers receive work from an employee, they benefit not merely from economic, but from *human* activity. Because the work-relationship turns on human activity, wages must be paid on the basis of the worker's humanity; they must betoken the subjective dimension of work. The Judeo-Christian tradition, and various other moral traditions, insist that employees, as persons, are entitled to

---

19. In the tradition of Catholic social thought, the principle of need is an expression of the principle of the common destination of goods. As Msgr. John A. Ryan puts it, "...the laborer's right to a Living Wage is merely the concrete expression of the general right...to obtain on reasonable terms as much of the common bounty of nature as will enable him to live decently" (*A Living Wage*, p. 237). The fruitful resources of the earth are the common heritage or fund of the human community. Hence, *e.g.*, Aquinas (*Summa Theologiae* IIa IIae q. 66, a. 2) denies that the destitute parent who takes, without paying for it, food to feed his/her starving children is a thief (cf. Ryan, *op. cit.*, pp. 69-70). A system which fails to direct property to the relief of urgent need is structurally deficient and itself needs fundamental reform.

receive compensation sufficient to lead a human life with dignity: sufficient, that is, to allow the development— ultimately, the flourishing—of the very humanity they have expressed in their work for their employer. Employees "surrender" their time and energy, and so cannot use them for another purpose. As Robert Kennedy explains, "What is especially important is that the employee has nothing else with which to earn his living, and so his productive energies are truly precious to him."[20] The wage is a way—for most, *the* way—of providing for human need.[21]

The principle of need, then, rests on the notion that the full and proper development of human personality requires material goods sufficient for the cultivation of the person's faculties.[22] Because work is necessary for the preservation of one's life, and for the procreation and education of offspring, compensation ought to entail a wage sufficient to support workers and their families in a relatively comfortable life, furnished with adequate food, clothing, housing, transportation, insurance, education, leisure and pension.[23]

---

20. Robert Kennedy (unpublished manuscript); Kennedy notes further, "The opportunity cost of choosing one employer over another can have drastic consequences which affect not only one's possessions, but potentially one's very life and the lives of one's family."

21. I am indebted to Ernest Pierucci for the argument of this paragraph; cf. Pieper's contrast between Stalin and Pius XI on human need and the wage (*op. cit.*, p. 53).

One should note that the principle of need may also be developed in light of the requirements of the employee's vocation. In the Catholic social tradition, the argument in this connection has usually taken form in the principle of the family wage, *i.e.*, of a wage adequate to sustain a family, but it may be more broadly applicable. The latter principle may be restated as the principle that the wage should allow an employee to fulfill the vocation of the head of a household to provide for spouse and children. The principle, then, is that income from one's full-time employment should suffice to fulfill the demands of one's vocation, including—but not limited to—one's familial responsibilities. So conceived, this principle appears as an alternative to the medieval idea that one's income ought to be commensurate to one's station in society. In modern, developed economies, of course, "station" has given way to (economic) "class," determined by income. The concept of vocation, then, may restore to the modern economy an analogue of "station" (cf. Michael Naughton and Robert Kennedy, "Executive Compensation: An Evaluation from the Catholic Social Tradition," *Social Justice Review* (Summer, 1993)).

22. Cf. Patrick W. Gearty, *The Economic Thought of Monsignor John A. Ryan* (Washington, D.C.: The Catholic University of America Press, 1953), p. 304.

23. Rates of compensation for full-time employees that fall below this threshold are, at the least, morally suspect, and are probably illegitimate, whether the source of the injustice is personal (an unjust employer) or structural (an unjust system). One can conceive a situation in which, temporarily, an employer might legitimately pay his full-time employees less than a living wage, if economic constraints beyond his control dictate that the resources to pay more are unavailable. John XXIII seems to suggest (*Mater et magistra*, n. 72) that such conditions could suspend application of the norms of justice. See Msgr. John A. Ryan's esti-

It is important to note at this juncture that the principle of need is independent of the "worth," "value" or "equivalent" of the work done. For, the principle is rooted in the subjective dimension of work, in the dignity of the worker, who is created in the image of God. Human labor, to repeat, cannot be exhausted, and so cannot be compensated, by its economic value. On the other hand, from the strategic perspective, labor, as a factor of production, is evaluated purely on an economic, value-added basis.[24] This contrast, as we will see, complicates the determination of a just wage.[25]

A living or just wage, then, is *the minimum amount due to every independent wage-earner by the mere fact that he or she is a human being with a life to maintain and a personality to develop.*[26]

Problems. For the U.S., inquiry into the living wage turns up a mixed picture. The U.S. has one of the highest standards of living in the world, because it generates some of the highest real wages in the world. In many cases, the market wage in the U.S. has proven an efficient instrument for providing living wages, especially for better educated or highly skilled employees, who have generally achieved wage-levels that more than adequately meet their basic needs. Latterly, in the 1980s and '90s, the demand for technical and professional skills boosted these employees' wages even higher.

However, less educated and lower-skilled employees suffered greatly during the same period: The real hourly wages of young men with twelve or fewer years of schooling dropped by some 20 percent from 1979-1989.[27] Displacement of unskilled work by technology, lower-wage for-

---

mate of a living wage for families (*A Living Wage*, Chp. VII), and Pope Leo XIII, *Rerum novarum*, n. 62.

24. Cf. Ryan, *A Living Wage*, pp. 97ff. (especially p. 100), and Ryan's debate with Cardinal Zigliara (*ibid.*, pp. 114-117).

25. Cf. *ibid.*, p. 15. Since ours is a consumer-oriented, as opposed to producer-oriented, economy, wage policy tends to become a function of the drive to lower prices.

26. This paper cannot, and does not pretend to, examine the full, complex range of questions implicated in a living wage: whether all jobs require living wages, and if not, which do and which do not require them? what role belongs to the state in determining living wages? what role does international competition play in determining the living wage? *etc.*

27. Richard B. Freeman, ed., *Working under Different Rules*, pp. 32-33. Despite such statistics, income per household is up, because hours worked per household are up owing to dual-income families, multiple jobs per earner, or increased hours per job. In 1973, *e.g.*, Germans and Americans worked the same number of hours per job; by 1992, Americans worked *one month* per year more than Germans (cf. Freeman, *op. cit.*, p. 3). Although the U.S. has achieved a high standard of living, Americans may have done so at the expense of the qual-

eign competition, and declining wage-supports from unions and government combined to leave the supply of unskilled workers greater than the demand for them. As a result, wages have declined,[28] leaving unskilled workers lower-paid *and* less secure in the jobs they hold.[29] Whether one earns a living wage in the U.S., then, depends largely on the level of one's skills and education. The relation between skills and education, on the one hand, and earning power, on the other, touches upon the foundational institutions of society: family, schools, government. Our concern with the relation here is restricted to how organizations have dealt with the issue of training, and in particular with how organizations in the U.S. tend to distribute opportunities for training.

Patterns in the distribution of training and development opportunities

---

ity of life: working more, spending less time with family, in churches, in schools and at other civic undertakings. In the tradition of Catholic social thought, a living wage is understood as a family wage based upon one earner, not two. Wage rates which force both spouses to become wage-earners work against familial stability and social cohesion (cf. *Laborem exercens*, n. 19.1). By contrast, *e.g.*: "In Japanese companies, each person's total situation will influence the amount of his income. The number of family members, his housing needs, the distance from his home to the plant, and other person-centered factors are given consideration" (Arthur M. Whitehill, *Japanese Management: Tradition and Transition* (New York: Routledge, 1991), p. 173).

28. While U.S. workers in high-wage jobs do better than their counterparts in Germany and Japan, workers in low-wage jobs—less skilled, less educated workers—in the U.S. do worse (cf. Freeman, *op. cit.*, p. 13, with the table, p. 38). U.S. wage inequality increased in 1980s and '90s, gains to the top 20% of earners far out-pacing gains to the bottom 20%. This trend has much to do with decentralization of the labor market and wage-setting practices, weak unions, a low minimum wage, the shift from manufactures to services, as well as relatively weak government protection for labor as compared to Europe (cf. Freeman, *op. cit.*, pp. 30, 45). While, then, the U.S. has experienced relatively low unemployment, compared to Europe, it has experienced greater under-employment and wage inequality. The bottom line: during the 1990s, low-wage Americans saw lower living standards "than low-wage workers in virtually all other advanced countries," while the rich are far better off in the U.S. than they are in other advanced countries (Richard Freeman and Lisa M. Lynch, "Payoffs to Alternative Training Strategies at Work" in Freeman, *op. cit.*, p. 226. *NB*: Freeman's and Lynch's comparisons use purchasing power parity to measure the value of foreign currencies).

29. Again, the reasons for increasing income disparity among American workers are varied and complex. For example, the premium earned by American college- or university-educated workers over those with a secondary education only rose from 37% in the late 1970s to 57% in 1989 (cf. "Rich man, poor man," *The Economist* (24 July, 1993), p. 71. *NB*: statistics were taken from OECD forecasts). Again, less skilled workers in Europe have suffered less than their American counter-parts because they have greater union representation. See Dean Baker's online report, "The U.S. Wage Gap and the Decline of Manufacturing" (http.//www.uswa.org/heartland/2manuf.htm).

to employees of U.S. firms seriously affect prospects for a living wage. In U.S. organizations, these opportunities go disproportionately to managerial or professional employees with university or college degress. One study reported that U.S. organizations are "...three to four times more likely to offer workshops on stress management or how to run meetings than to train laborers seeking to upgrade their positions."[30] Another study found that "...while 17% of executive, administrative and managerial personnel received training provided by their employers in a given year, the comparable figure for machine operators was 4%."[31] A survey by the Hay Group revealed that more than 60% of employees felt their company did not provide them with the training necessary to advance.[32] On top of this injury is added the insult of executives going off for training to exotic locales, enjoying luxurious accommodations.

By comparison with German and Japanese corporate training programs, U.S. efforts look elitist.[33] German firms invest over twice the amount in worker training, and approximately *seventeen* times the amount in training per apprentice, that U.S. firms invest. Consequently, the German work-force is one of the most productive, most disciplined and skilled work-forces in the world, as well as the highest-paid. In Japan, new workers in certain industries receive "...approximately 300 hours of training, while their U.S. counterparts receive only 48 hours of training."[34] Although exemplary U.S. companies, such as Motorola, require all employees to undergo one week of training yearly, they seem to be the exceptions which prove the rule.[35]

This brief description of patterns in corporate training suggests that one of the chief economic problems for workers is not so much the rigors of the market economy, but rather their marginal relation to the

---

30. Jeffrey Pfeffer, *California Management Review* (Winter, 1994), p. 20.

31. *Ibid*; see also Freeman and Lynch, *op. cit.*, p. 71.

32. Cf. Flannery, Hofrichter and Platten, *op. cit.*, p. 15.

33. It should be pointed out that workers in the U.S. tend to receive much of their training informally, learning through doing. While informal learning initially raises productivity, in the long run it fails to have a substantial effect. "Three recent studies show that formal training has a high pay-off in the United States, but that the pay-offs differ by type of training" (Freeman and Lynch, *op. cit.*, p. 82).

34. Freeman and Lynch, *op. cit.*, p. 74. German apprentices are paid less than their U.S. counterparts, allowing the more intensive, more sustained training which increases the Germans' future wages more rapidly than the Americans'.

35. Cf. E.E. Lawler, S.A. Mohrman and G.E. Leford, Jr., *Creating High Performance Organizations* (San Francisco: Jossey-Bass Publishers, 1995), p. 15.

knowledge which drives the market. Many workers today are crippled participants in the market and production process because they are short the requisite skills and knowledge.[36] Although degrading conditions still exist in the textile, agricultural, and other sectors of the economy, a root of sub-living wages is sub-marketable knowledge or skill.[37]

Solution: Skill/Knowledge-Based Pay.[38] In light of this situation, and of managers' limited spheres of influence, an effective way to promote a living wage is through redesigning work so that it requires greater skill and knowledge. In general, the more highly skilled the work, the easier it is to pay a living wage.[39] Skill-based pay is attractive, because it fosters conditions under which companies can pay a living wage without suf-

---

36. John Paul II traces this state of affairs to a fundamental shift from a land-based economy to an information-based economy, a point anticipated by John XXIII in 1961. He writes, "Work becomes ever more fruitful and productive to the extent that people become more knowledgeable of the productive potentialities of the earth and more profoundly cognizant of the needs of those for whom their work is done" (*Centesimus annus*, n. 31). John Paul observes that "possession of know-how, technology and skill" have become more important than the ownership of land in developed nations. Hence, the kind of work one has to offer increases in importance: those who are unskilled can no longer afford to remain so, and those who are skilled need continually to update their skills.

37. John Paul II observes, "Many people, perhaps the majority today, do not have the means which would enable them to take their place in an effective and humanly dignified way within a productive system in which work is truly central. They have no possibility of acquiring the basic knowledge which would enable them to express their creativity and develop their potential. They have no way of entering the network of knowledge and intercommunication which would enable them to see their qualities appreciated and utilized" (*Centesimus annus*, n. 33). Although such workers may not be literally exploited, they are nonetheless marginalized. They are, for any of a variety of reasons, excluded from information, but whatever the reason, the result is a poorly paid work-force in a non-participative organization.

38. See Robert L. Rose, "A Productivity Push at Wabash National Puts Firm on a Roll," *The Wall Street Journal* (September 7, 1995). Skill/knowledge-based systems of compensation focus on the development of three classes of skills: vertical or "upward" skills, usually exercised by management (*e.g.*, inventory or quality control, scheduling, team leadership); horizontal or "trade" skills (*e.g.*, mastering the various jobs upstream and downstream on a production line); "depth" or technical skills, such as are stressed in apprenticeship programs, which look to "deepen" skill in a particular function (*e.g.*, carpentry, electric, machine maintenance; accounting, tax reporting). See E. E. Lawler, *Strategic Pay* (San Francisco: Jossey-Bass Publishers, 1990), pp. 155ff., and E. E. Lawler and G. E. Ledford, "Skill-Based Pay," *Personnel* 62, 9 (1985), p. 30.

39. For example, high-tech companies, who typically employ a highly skilled workforce, generate the highest revenues per employee; conversely, food market companies, who typically employ a low-skilled workforce, generate some of the lowest revenues per employee. Of course, if revenues are not available to pay a living wage, the point is moot.

fering net competitive disadvantages.[40] Within the means available to them, managers can help less skilled, less educated workers achieve living wages by training and developing them in tandem with redesigning their work. If firms can "smarten" the job, through training and skill development, they make employees more marketable by making them more efficient and productive, results which, in their turn, promote organizational conditions favorable to paying a full, living wage.[41] One limited study conducted in the U.S. found that company-based training increased wages from between 4.4% and 11%, with a corresponding 17% increase in productivity.[42]

Skill-based pay not only increases wages, but may also enhance the subjective rewards of work. When employees participate in their own skill-development, they begin to take ownership over their work. Skill-development, *e.g.*, promotes employee self-management. By training employees in necessary skills, organizations "push," in effect, knowledge, information and decision-making down to "lower-levels" of the organization, a practice of the classical principle of subsidiarity. As subsidiary partners in the enterprise, employees tend to view their work as an expression of themselves, while their increased knowledge of the organization leads them to understand their work "in the round," rather than as a "flat," isolated activity. The result is a *social* development which increases *organizational* effectiveness, *viz.*, employees coming to understand

40. Unsurprisingly, knowledge/skill-based systems of compensation involve trade-offs among various advantages and disadvantages. E. E. Lawler summarizes the typical net result ("The New Pay: A Strategic Approach," *Compensation and Benefits Review* (1 July, 1995), p. 17): "In most cases, skill-based pay tends to produce somewhat higher pay levels for individuals, but these costs are usually offset by greater work-force flexibility and performance. Flexibility often leads to lower staffing levels and less absenteeism or turnover, both of which may drop because employees appreciate the opportunity to utilize and be paid for a wide range of skills." In *Strategic Pay*, Lawler reviews the catalogue of benefits (pp. 160f.) and disadvantages (pp. 166f.) which tend to accrue to skill/knowledge-based pay.

41. Freeman and Lynch, *op. cit.*, p. 77. Skill-based pay carries the obvious danger of producing pay-rates which may increase faster than gains from increased productivity or enhanced product quality. Equally obviously, management will play a critical role in measuring out resources. That role may involve holding wages at the margins of "living" levels initially, while allowing accelerated increases in them as productivity and quality gains accrue in the medium- to long-run (cp. our remarks on German apprentice-training, n. 35, above).

42. *Ibid.*, pp. 83-85. To date, such studies work from small samples, and despite their encouraging results, organizations seem to be deterred from adopting skill-based systems by doubts over whether the initial, relatively high investment in employees can be justified, given rates of employee turnover (particularly in a highly mobile society) and the relatively long run required to recoup the investment.

and to undertake their work as a community of action.[43] Moreover, employee participation in-skill-based pay apportions part of the burden of achieving living wages on the employees themselves: if employees fail to seize the opportunity for self-advancement, then they must accept the consequences.

One creative way to marry the desire to pay a living wage with the advantages of skill-based pay is by creating what Reell Precision Manufacturing calls a "target wage." At Reell, a Salary Review Committee establishes a target wage based on a rough idea of a reasonable, local standard of living. In 1996, this target or living wage amounted to $10.91 an hour ($22,500 a year). Some employees hired at RPM fall below this target wage, owing to their relative lack of experience or relatively weak skills. Market factors dictate that these employees be paid as little as $6.80 an hour. In response, Reell has enriched affected jobs so that the firm's lowest-paid employees can advance rapidly to the target wage.[44] Reell has redesigned its manufacturing processes to entail more skill and decision-making on the part of employees, creating organizational conditions which demand less supervision, speed set-up times and reduce the need for quality inspection. Reell's program reduces overall costs, allowing the company to pay the "target wage." The institution of the target

43. See the "personalist argument" of John Paul II's *Laborem exercens*; see also Flannery *et al.*, *People, Performance and Pay*. The importance of initiative on the personal and small-group levels is rooted in the principle of subsidiarity, which asserts that it is an injustice for larger associations to arrogate to themselves activities that can be performed by smaller associations or individual persons. The role of larger associations is, rather, to augment the freedom of smaller groups and of individuals by supplying helps which exceed the latters' resources. Work is a means by which persons perfect their human powers. The larger economic organization—firm or national marketplace—must represent "in form and substance" a "true community," in which employees are assisted toward their human ends, are treated according to their human dignity, and are moved to contribute to the achievement of common goods (see John XXIII, *Mater et magistra*, n. 65). The workplace, conceived and conducted as a human community, will incorporate subsidiary structures through which employees not only make marketable goods, but achieve with managers and the ownership the good of justice, betokened by a just wage.

44. A major innovation, though not originally conceived as a way of addressing wages, is Reell's redesign of its manufacturing line. From a Command-Direct-Control (CDC) system, in which managers and engineers decided and directed the design and activity of the assembly area, Reell moved to a Teach-Equip-Trust (TET) partnership with workers: employees are taught, equipped and trusted to run their own assembly processes. Such concrete practices give substance to Reell's stated policy: "It is our *intent*, under normal business conditions, to pay people hired below this RPM Living Wage *accelerated* increases (as compared to other co-workers not below the Living Wage) until the Living Wage is reached" (*Reell Precision Manufacturing Corporation Salary System Overview*).

wage, it should be stressed, was informed by the founders' deep sense of stewardship for the growth and well-being of employees.

Christian social tradition, especially as it is articulated in Catholic social teaching, does not hold Reell bound to pay employees in excess of a market wage, even if the market wage falls below a living wage. To do so would put Reell—and all of the firm's employees—at risk of failure, and would in any case encourage in employees an unhealthy dependence on Reell for a standard of living they could not otherwise achieve in the marketplace. Reell is morally responsible for working with employees to increase their skills, so to move them toward the target wage, which Reell has carefully fashioned as a viable, economic wage; employees are no less morally responsible for learning and working diligently. A genuine, practical wisdom permits Reell to meet both fundamental, strategic demands —efficiency, productivity, quality—and the human needs of the firm's employees. Reell's experience clearly illustrates that the living wage is no static rule of thumb; it is, rather, an end-means—i.e., a moral—dynamic, in which the desire for justice enlists managerial and fiscal prudence to create a concrete, on-going practice—in Reell's case, the target wage.[45]

We need to pause here in order to evaluate a certain logical tension arising from our insisting at once on the *principle of need* at the root of the very notion of the living wage and the emphasis we have placed on *skill development* as a condition for the achievement of just wages. We asserted that a just or living wage rests, not on the work incident to it, but on the human dignity of the worker. At the same time, we argued that the value of skill/knowledge-based pay consists in enhancing the employee's economic ability to justify a living wage. Some may argue that our reliance on skill/knowledge-based pay surrenders the principle of need to market pressures, and ends merely in a novel way of treating human labor as a commodity.

It is important to reiterate that the argument concerns the *manager's* sphere of influence, the means at the manager's disposal for promoting a living wage. Given the competitive price system to which nearly all managers are subject, the most direct, effective means of promoting a living

---

45. Managers and entrepreneurs, then, have a moral duty to organize and design jobs productive enough to support a living wage. This duty should not be misconceived as though it were opposed to their recognized duty to enhance the economic value of the firm. As Reell's experience suggests, employees trained to capability for partnership in the achievement of just wages also increase their relative contribution to the economic value of the firm.

wage that managers command within the organization involve: (1) developing employees' skills, making employees more efficient, productive and cost-effective; (2) structuring work to take advantage of employees' enhanced skills.

In justice, managers must pay a living wage, but who wills the end must will the means: apart from prudent, concrete means of sustaining them, "just wages" amount to an empty intention, an exercise in "moralism" which cannot deliver on its promise. For this reason, employers are not—because they cannot be—solely responsible for achieving living wages. In a real sense, any individual firm's living wage can only be an *instance* of a *social* achievement founded in the cooperation of employer, employees, and "indirect employers": suppliers, customers, trade associations, unions, financial institutions...and the agencies of government. For, apart from a comprehensive commitment—a social commitment— to the living wage, those who determine to pay a living wage in competitive, highly price-sensitive markets, risk economic disadvantages that cannot long be borne.

Yet, it is precisely the competitive price system which weds managers to an exclusively strategic view of pay, and leads them to run the risk of instrumentalizing their workers. To be sure, proponents of the strategic view often acknowledge the importance of a living wage: they know, *e.g.*, that low base-pay "...can cause significant problems in recruiting and retaining the best and brightest individuals...[or] an internal culture of low esteem and...a feeling that the organization in general is second best and lacks the resources to do a first-rate job."[46] But the same strategic logic may decree that if jobs require "...a low level of skills and enjoy a large labor supply, then a strategy of high pay may not be appropriate...," for, "increasing labor costs may produce a minimum number of benefits."[47] Benefits for whom? The strategic approach defines "benefits" in terms of contributions to the strategic goals of the organization; *in fine*, employees are not other than "organizational resources," means and not ends. While, therefore, strategic thinking excels at increasing productivity and efficiency, it discounts moral and spiritual imagination. It is difficult to believe that Reell Precision Manufacturing could have developed the target wage on strategic grounds alone, or had the firm's leadership not first desired just relationships with Reell's employees.

46. Lawler, *Strategic Pay*, p. 185.
47. Lawler, "The New Pay: A Strategic Approach," p. 18.

2. An Equitable Wage

The Principle of Contribution. If full-time, adult employees' compensation fails to provide for their basic needs, something is fundamentally wrong with the organization, with the larger economic and political structure, or with both. Still, just compensation supposes a complex system within a complex organization. It cannot be determined by one principle, such as need, alone. The principle of need is necessary for determining a just wage, but alone it is insufficient, since it accounts only for employees as consumers and fails to address their productive contributions to the enterprise. By their painstaking effort and sacrifice—as well as by their skill, education and experience—some employees contribute more, and more of themselves, to the common enterprise than others; in distributive justice, they are due more pay.

The principle of contribution, in its guise as the demand for equity, is no less deeply grounded in the Catholic social tradition than the principle of need. Thus, *e.g.*, St. Thomas Aquinas noted that a failure of distributive justice is responsible for quarrels and complaints arising when workers are paid the same wages for unequal work, or unequal wages for equal work.[48] But indeed, on a purely pragmatic basis, there is nothing more harmful to morale than pay by job title, rather than by contribution to organizational success.

Although equal in their dignity—and so, equal in their right to the fulfillment of their human needs—people are decidedly unequal in the efforts they expend, the sacrifices they make, and the productive capacities they deploy. A living wage, while the foundation, does not complete the structure of the just wage: the just wage must also be an equitable wage.[49] Honoring workers through the wage relation also entails recognizing their talents and efforts. An equitable wage, then, is *the measure of the contribution of an employee's productivity and effort within the context of*

---

48. St. Thomas Aquinas, *Commentary on Aristotle's Nicomachean Ethics*, p. 296; cf. p. 342.

49. Cf. Ryan, *A Living Wage*, p. 75. John XXIII (*Mater et magistra*) added "equity" to "justice" in order to tie the discussion more directly to compensation's second ground, *viz.*, what portion of the whole good made or achieved derives from the contribution of the worker. A wage based on "justice and equity" should derive not only from consumptive needs (commutative justice), but also from how the worker has contributed to the expansion of economies, that is, from what equity the worker has contributed (distributive justice).

the existing profits and resources of the organization.[50] The difficulty with equity is to find a measure which is neither narrowly mechanical nor rigidly quantitative, nor yet too broadly impressionistic or vague.

Problems. One of the most contentious and explosive issues involving business organizations today, an issue which calls the equitability of the wage-system into question, is the wide—and widening—disparity between employee and executive compensation.[51] There is no contention over the main cause: it lies in the allocation of bonuses, stock options and grants, restricted stock and cash pay-outs to executives.[52] The question of who participates in these various incentives raises the prior question of who is responsible for companies' success. Some executives tend to *pay* like cowboys, but *talk* like monks: they sermonize on the importance of employees' contributions, but pay as though the executive is the Lone Ranger of the bottom line. This is not to deny that executives should be paid according to the rarity and sophistication of their talent and decision-making abilities, but as Michael Novak points out, most of today's high compensatory rewards

---

50. Ernest Bartell, "*Laborem Exercens*: A Third World Perspective," in John W. Houck and Oliver Williams, eds., *Co-Creation and Capitalism* (Lanham, Maryland: University Press of America, 1983), p. 187; John A Ryan (cf. *Distributive Justice* (New York: Macmillan, 1942³), pp. 180-188) has systematically captured this link in his six canons of distributive justice.

51. Robert Reich captures a near-universal suspicion, "There is something wrong with rising profits, rising productivity and a soaring stock market, but employee compensation heading nowhere" (*Minneapolis Tribune*, November 1, 1995). Indeed, one *has to wonder* where excess profits are going when various stock markets are at all-time highs *and* employee wages are flat.

52. Incentives allocated to top corporate executives have raised executive pay to previously unheard-of levels, leaving—as the *Wall Street Journal* (April 11, 1996) put it—"everybody else further and further behind." The reason, before everything else: stock options; next, other forms of financial incentives: profit-sharing, performance bonuses, and so on. U.S. corporations have traditionally restricted such incentives to the top levels of the organizational hierarchy. *E.g.*, a Conference Board study of 491 companies found that 59% of them offered bonus plans to top executives, while only 11% offered employees profit-sharing plans; 8% offered all-employee bonuses, 3% group-productivity incentives, and less than 1% offered cost-control incentives (Rosabeth Koss Kantor, "The Attack on Pay," *Harvard Business Review* (March-April, 1987), p. 62). The extreme—but instructive—case is represented, perhaps, by United Airlines Chairman, Stephen M. Wolf. "Wolf collected $18.3 million in salary, bonus and stock incentive plans—a tidy sum for heading up a company whose profits fell by 71% in 1991. Put another way, that's 1,200 times what new flight attendants earned at United Airlines, Inc. in each of the last five years—a period when none of them got a raise" (John A. Byrne, "The Flap Over Executive Pay," *Business Week* (May 6, 1991), p. 93).

...do not go to inventors or discoverers, but rather to managers of large corporate enterprises, of which top managers are only small, if crucial, parts. There is something supremely social in their achievements. What they did, they did not do alone. Their achievement rests upon the intelligence, enterprise and creativity of many others in their firms—and upon the social system (the U.S. political economy) that made their efforts possible. It is wrong to reward them as if they were Lone Rangers.[53]

Or, as Dean Farlin points out, "Company performance rarely, if ever, hangs on the work of just one individual"[54] or of a few, for that matter.

Stock options and comparable incentives, we are told, motivate executives to perform. That rationale neatly highlights the problem: Executives don't "perform" in the required sense, organizations do. If the new "knowledge economy" entails the inability of individual managers at every level to master the range of various and specialized knowledge required for organizational success, top executives should be making less money, not more, since they no longer dominate a uniquely valuable niche in the hierarchy of talent.[55] With sad irony, the recent growth of ex-

53. Michael Novak, "The Executive Joneses," *Forbes* (May 29, 1989), p. 95. See Adolf A. Berle and Gardiner Means, *The Modern Corporation and Private Property*, Revised Edition (New York: Harcourt, Brace and World, 1968), pp. xii-xiii and 299-302, for the traditional reasoning behind allocating incentives primarily to executives, namely, that incentives substitute for the rewards (profits) of ownership in spurring management to care zealously for the economic well-being of joint-stock property. A recent study reported in the *Wall Street Journal* (March 23, 1993, p. 1), calls the traditional reasoning into question. Is suggests strongly that significant levels of stock ownership by executives has little effect on the economic order and health of the company. On the contrary, companies in which non-executive employees own more than 10% of the firm's stock do far better. What may not be true of executive ownership may indeed be true if a stake in the company's success is more broadly distributed among its employees.

54. Quoted in Erik Gunn and John Fauber, "Pay at Top is Raising Questions," *The Milwaukee Journal* (May 5, 1991), p. D12.

55. U.S. companies' failure to distribute financial incentives and rewards leads many American employees to dissever their job-performance from the exercise of creative effort, perseverance and other characteristics associated with high achievement. For example, Japanese and U.S. workers were asked in a poll who would profit from an increase in productivity and quality in their plants. Only 9% of the U.S. workers believed benefits would accrue to their efforts, compared to 93% of Japanese workers (cf. Robert Bachelder, "Japan and the U.S.: The Economics of Equity," *The Christian Century* (August 26, 1987), pp. 719-723). U.S. CEOs who aspire to enhance organizational teamwork or to foster a sense of corporate purpose cannot expect to motivate managers or workers when their own compensation is viewed as an unjustified excess (cf. Sheldon Friedman, "The Compelling Case for

ecutive salaries parallels the introduction of "knowledge workers" and "work teams" calculated to shift responsibility and decision-making to employees at all levels within the organization.[56]

It should come as no surprise that employees compare their pay, and the *bases* of their pay, to those of occupants of the higher rungs on the corporate ladder. Executives who "hoard" incentive programs for themselves and their immediate colleagues create conditions ripe for cynicism, envy and poor morale. When the distributive rhetoric of a corporate mission statement clashes with functionally oligarchic pay practices, a company will prove culturally dysfunctional at its core, never to realize its full potential.[57]

Solution: Pay for Performance.[58] Pushing pay-for-performance incentives downward and outward within the organization can facilitate a more equitable system of compensation by inviting employees to share in the organization's rewards *and* in its risks. In fact, one study found that 63% of employees stated that they would like "...to see their pay more closely tied to their company's annual performance, and even an higher percentage— 75%—indicated they'd like to see their pay more closely tied to the annual performance of the operating unit they work in."[59] Just as employees grasp (and resent) the inequity of restricted incentive-pay, so they un-

---

Cutting Executive Compensation," *California Management Review* 77 (March, 1988), pp. 61-62).

56. It should be stressed that no organization can become a true community of action based upon a Taylorian view of talent. Like any true community, the organization as an economic community must exercise as fully as possible the talents, skills and potentialities of every employee. Otherwise, the organization becomes a mere aggregation of individuals, without a common bond or real common purpose beyond collecting a regular paycheck.

57. "Resentment over pay gaps, in fact, was revealed in a recent study by William H. Mercer, Inc., New York" (Donald J. McNerney, *HR Focus* (October, 1995), p. 5). The relatively few companies which push pay-for-performance incentives farther down into the organization are bedeviled by wide disparities. When labor and middle managers receive 2-3% merit increases, while executives receive 20-40% increases, on the basis of performance by the organization overall, "incentive" begins to look to the former like ridicule from above. As one quality-control supervisor put it, such disparities "...mock the concept of teamwork needed to compete in today's markets" (cf. Michael A. Verespej, "Pay for Skills: Its Time Has Come," *Industry Week* (June 15, 1992), pp. 22-30).

58. Pay-for-performance plans involve three basic variations in scope: (1) individual (*e.g.*, merit pay, bonuses, executive stock options, *etc.*); (2) team or departmental (*e.g.*, gainsharing); divisional or organizational (*e.g.*, profit-sharing, stock ownership/ESOPs); compensation varies by formula according to the performance of the unit, up to the entire firm, which falls under the plans scope.

59. Verespej, *loc. cit.* It should be noted that another survey found that 72% of blue-collar, and 56% of white collar, workers would prefer straight wages over any type of incentive

derstand (and accept) that asking them to do more, to be better equipped *and* to share in the risks and rewards of their company's performance is equitable.

Gainsharing is one way of building equity into a firm's wage-system.[60] Gainsharing is based on the improved productivity of the individual worker or work team. Since profits and productivity are not always increased in tandem, gainsharing establishes a direct connection between workers' productivity and their pay.[61] It is based upon a formula which connects increased individual or team productivity to increases in compensation, irrespective of the company's overall performance. In short, gainsharing rewards those who make improvements at any organizational level, thereby increasing equity within the organization.[62]

Successful gainsharing plans turn on two factors: formula and organizational culture. Gainsharing plans must employ clear and concise criteria, so that employees have no doubt about what they have to accomplish in order to receive bonuses; the gainsharing formula should measure performance to the desired standards/goals with clarity and precision. Gainsharing bonuses, unlike bonuses under a profit-sharing plan, are allocated quarterly, sometimes monthly, to reinforce success with reward.[63]

---

plan (cf. *Changing Pay Practices: New Developments in Employee Compensation*, Bureau of National Affairs, 1988).

60. Gainsharing differs significantly from the more familiar profit-sharing. Profit-sharing is based upon improvements in the firm's overall profitability: employees receive a share of any resulting, residual profits. Structurally, therefore, profit-sharing is subject to business conditions outside employees' control: their efforts at increasing productivity or controlling costs need not translate into increased profitability, but may be negated at the bottom line by a changing economic climate, the effects of government regulation or deregulation, depreciation procedures, or a host of other factors. Moreover, profit-sharing operates on a "total system incentive approach" (cf. Brian Graham Moore and Timothy L. Ross, *Gainsharing: Plans for Improving Performance* (Washington, D.C.: Bureau of National Affairs, 1990), p. 26). That is to say, profit-sharing operates on the supposition that "a rising tide lifts all boats": it rewards or penalizes *all* members of the organization according to the profitability (or the reverse) of the whole. Profit-sharing, then, ties employees' immediate job-performance indirectly or mediately to financial rewards.

By contrast, gainsharing rewards the enhanced performance of production units or individuals over a shorter term and regardless their performance's effects on overall profitability. Gainsharing, then, ties employees' ongoing, immediate performance directly to financial rewards.

61. Cf. Lawler, *Strategic Pay*, pp. 110ff.

62. *Ibid.*, Chp. 9. There is, however, the difficulty of rewarding support staff whose work allows a unit to function well, but does not fall within its function.

63. Some theorists call this connection a "strong line of sight," since it make apparent to employees a strong correlation between cause (hard, "smart" work) and effect (higher pay).

Herman Miller, designers and manufacturers of furniture, employs the Scanlon gainsharing plan.[64] Employees negotiate with management to determine goals in four areas: (1) effective customer service; (2) effective use of money; (3) effective use of materials; (4) effective use of labor. The plan does not necessarily focus on increasing output, but on reducing production costs as well as on improving the quality of products. The latter is a crucial point, since many individual incentive plans focused on increased output show disappointing effects on product quality.

No successful gainsharing plan can function purely as a "productivity technique" operating with the "right formula." Its success will owe much to the "deep" culture of a view of the human person which shapes the organization's purposes. We return to the subjective dimension of work: successful gainsharing should be framed in light of, and should be strongly connected to, the company's larger purposes, particularly as these relate to human development.

Herman Miller, for example, sees its gainsharing plan as embedded in an organizational culture which fosters the subjective dimension of work by creating conditions of *participation, transparency, ownership*, and *equity*.[65] Employee *participation* plays a critical role in the value, effective-

---

64. The Scanlon Plan, the oldest and most popular gainsharing plan, originated in the 1930s, when Joseph Scanlon, a local union president, attempted to prevent the shut-down of a steel mill. The Scanlon plan rests on the idea that participation in, and improvement of, the firm must be rewarded financially, if participation and improvements are to be sustained. It has been used as a framework for labor/management relations. The plan provides a context in which a common objective, organizational effectiveness, is achieved by worker participation, and reinforced by compensation based on success. Basically, the plan projects the costs of production for a given month and, if savings over the projection are achieved, awards workers a percentage of them. Contemporary versions distribute approximately 75% of gains to employees, and the balance to the firm.

Not to be neglected is the fundamental importance of worker participation and trust to the success of gainsharing (cf. Lawler, *Strategic Pay*, pp. 157-162). If workers are to improve the organization's effectiveness, management must trust them with information vital to operations, and workers must trust management to apportion gains per agreement. Such trust demands that equitable practices characterize the firm throughout. This means, *e.g.*, an end to the trappings of managerial/executive privilege: special parking lots, dining rooms, health clubs, *etc.* Their removal constitutes, perhaps, only small gestures, but potent ones nonetheless for expressing an organization's commitment to thoroughgoing equity.

65. Gainsharing is considered a good idea not simply because it has organizational advantages or enhances effectiveness, but because it is the right way to treat people. It is seen as returning to the employee much of the control and income-enhancement opportunity that began to decline with the advent of scientific management and modern managerialism.... It is, therefore, not simply a compensation system or even a way of paying people more fairly. Rather, it is seen as a better way of organizing and managing people. For a few companies

ness and acceptability of gainsharing programs, because it constitutes an agreement that the program is fair and equitable. Participation requires in turn a high degree of *transparency*: information must be regularly, openly disseminated throughout the organization. Herman Miller spends one day each month informing employees on the status of productivity, profits and employees' suggestions. The connection participation and transparency forge between their performance and their financial reward has increased employees' awareness of the company's financial status, and has partially flattened the organization's decision-making structure.

Herman Miller also provides an employee stock *ownership* plan, which has contributed to the growth of an "ownership culture": employees are encouraged to regard the company as their company; hence, at Herman Miller, authority neither tends to derive from "opaque" sources such as seniority, nor tends to appear arbitrary, but tends to derive from demonstrated competence, knowledge and skill. Finally, Herman Miller observes an *equity* pay ratio: the highest-paid employee, usually the CEO, cannot be paid more than 20 times the pre-tax income of the firm's manufacturing employees.[66] When, in the 1980s, compensation committees were designing golden parachutes for top executives, Herman Miller's former CEO, Max De Pree, designed *silver* parachutes for *all* employees, protecting the whole workforce—not just a select few—from raiders.[67]

Herman Miller's gainsharing program fosters equitable pay precisely because it is embedded in an organizational culture that takes seriously the subjective dimensions of employees and their work. Gainsharing can avoid degenerating into a manipulative instrument in the hands of management only if it is regulated under an institutional culture committed

---

—including Herman Miller, a Michigan furniture and design company, and Lincoln Electric in Cleveland—gainsharing is the core management principle for the whole organization" (Kanter, *op. cit.*, p. 81). See Laura Nash, *Believers in Business* (Nashville: Thomas Nelson Publishers, 1994), pp. 148ff., on Herman Miller.

66. Byrne *et al.*, *op. cit.*, p. 48. Ben and Jerry's, the ice cream concern, observed a similar distribution ratio, originally set at 5:1, then increased to 7:1, then dropped altogether. Critical to the success of Herman Miller had been the leadership of the CEO, Max De Pree, who embraced the goal of building a "covenant" within the organization. Thus, while Herman Miller's wage structure aims to distribute compensation equitably, it also provides incentives for employees to broaden their skills and knowledge not only as means to higher earnings, but as a means to personal development and deeper satisfaction in their work.

67. Cf. Charles R. Day, "Kerm Campbell 'We Need to Change the Meaning of Management,'" *Industry Week* (November 7, 1994), p. 39.

to forging just relationships through participation, transparency, owner-ship and equity.

3. A Sustainable Wage

The Principle of Economic Order. If compensation were only a mat-ter of paying employees according to their needs and contributions, a just wage would be relatively easy to implement. But pay is not only income for the worker, it is also a cost to the employer which has a significant im-pact on the economic order of the organization. A just wage cannot be determined "without reference to the quantity and quality of available resources" or to the effects present wages and incentives will work on fu-ture resources.[68] The principle of economic order examines the employer's ability to pay wages that are sustainable, that allow for the economic health of the organization as a whole. An ecological principle operates in pay systems: actions provoke chains of consequences running in every di-rection, throughout the organization. As a prime regulator of a business, profits play a critical role in the determination of any pay plan. Apart from reliable estimates as to how a living and equitable wage will affect the economic order of the organization, the just wage becomes a high-sounding—practically empty—moralism.[69]

Problems. Throughout, this paper has criticized the strategic view of pay as a form of instrumentalism. The critique, to repeat, does not imply wholesale rejection of strategic thinking: the argument is, rather, that pro-ponents of strategic pay fail to recognize the limits of strategic thinking's understanding of pay. In order to articulate these limits, an important dis-tinction must be drawn between techniques and virtues;[70] in its turn, this distinction will help to integrate a strategic with a just understanding of pay.

---

68. Cf. John XXIII, *Mater et magistra*, n. 72.

69. For the organization is not merely an aggregate of individuals, but rather it is an *uni-tas ordinis*, an ordered unity; it has a mission, "a framework of rules by which the *ordo* and the *unitas* of the wills of the individuals are produced and their functions integrated into an organic whole" (Heinrich A. Rommen, *The State in Catholic Thought* (St. Louis: Herder Book Co., 1945), p. 184). Once this ordered unity becomes disengaged from the competi-tive environment in which it finds itself, no matter how good their intentions, organizations will fail.

70. Cf. Servais Pinckaers, *The Sources of Christian Ethics*, trans. Noble (Washington, D.C.: The Catholic University of America Press, 1995), pp. 83ff.; John Paul II, *Laborem ex-ercens* 5-6.

Strategy is a technique for adopting courses of action — planned or emergent — and for allocating resources, necessary for the long-term, economic viability of the organization. Since pay is a significant part of the organizational cost-structure, it needs to be designed so as to furnish a competitive advantage in the strategic direction of the company.[71] Still, however *necessary*, strategic thinking is *not sufficient* to understand the full reality of pay. It is necessary because it maps out the economic and productive implications of the organization's wage-system, and thereby provides a safeguard for the organization's economic order; strategic thinking is not sufficient because it lacks the moral imagination to foster right relationships among people. Left to itself, strategy avoids the deeply human question, "Does their pay help people to develop *as* people?" The adoption of strictly strategic and financial objectives reduces the latter question to secondary, instrumental status; the strategic logic such objectives generate ineluctably treats human beings as means, as human *resources*, and nothing more. Only objectives that take seriously the importance of justice in the context of human beings' social nature can serve to place people, as ends in themselves, in right relationships.

As technique, strategic thinking has advanced: witness the volume of writing in business strategy. Unfortunately, its ascendence has not been integrated with reflection on the demands of justice.[72] A virtue, such as justice, is habitual human action, ordered to a good/end, that renders the acting person good. Virtue thus qualifies the person comprehensively: "This person is just" means that right relations to others color every aspect of the person's activity. Technique qualifies a person only partially: "This person is productive" means only that some of the person's activities fulfill a prescribed function well. Strategic thinking deals with pay in technical — *viz.*, partial — terms: This pay-system is productive, or profitable, or...*etc.* Just wage theory deals comprehensively with the pay-relationship.[73] It does so because, while it does not discount strategic factors, it looks first and seriously to the subjective dimension of the person and of human work. Contrarily, so far as strategic thinking restricts the pay-relationship to a technical practice subordinated to economic goals,

71. Cf. P. A. Zingheim and J. R. Schuster, "Introduction: How Are the New Pay Tools Being Developed?," *Compensation and Benefits Review* (July-August, 1995), p. 10.

72. Cf. John Paul II, *Redemptor hominis*, n. 15; cf. also Freeman, Gilbert and Hartman, "Values and the Foundation of Strategic Management," *Journal of Business Ethics* 7 (1988), pp. 821-834.

73. Pinckaers, *op. cit.*, p. 84.

it subjects the person of the worker to a technical system measured by "economic value added," and "enslaves the human person through a lack of understanding of his moral dimension, to the detriment of human dignity."[74]

These are harsh words; an example may help to illustrate their bearing. H. J. Heinz Company instituted a management incentive plan (MIP) based on the company's strategic goal of "consistent growth in earnings."[75] Rewards and penalties assessed under the plan adhered strictly to the company's earnings-projections: when division management met their targets, they earned bonuses up to 40% of their salary; when they failed to meet their targets, they came under great scrutiny and pressure from corporate headquarters to rectify the situation.

The flat demand that they achieve "consistent growth in earnings" in an inconsistent marketplace pressured Heinz's divisional managers into extreme, at times illegal, accounting practices—such as transferring reported income and expenses from one fiscal year to the next—calculated to guarantee their rewards and to insulate them against corporate hectoring. Although Heinz touted a code of ethics, in practice employees responded not to what the company professed, but to what it rewarded: Heinz sent clear messages that rewards went to those who met targets, not to those who adhered to ethical or legal norms. In effect, Heinz created a system of incentives to a culture of economism, elevating consistent growth in earnings to the prime measure of "right"—rewarded—action, and penalizing those who failed to reach economic targets, even for legitimate reasons.

More can be learned about an incentive system from what it penalizes than from what it rewards. Heinz instituted a system of penalties that discouraged honest dealing, even with purely economic problems, and cast noneconomic goals—such as honesty in exposing dubious accounting practices—into a kind of limbo: they did not fall under the company's system of rewards; pursuing them might well be cause for penalty, should they appear inconsistent with the overriding strategic goal. When a company can muster only narrow strategic goals and economic self-interest as motivators and guides to decision-making, it must be content with the consequences of narrow, self-interested decisions.

Need it be said that an over-emphasis on quantifiable goals is hardly

---

74. Pinckaers, *op. cit.*, p. 87.

75. Cf. Matthews, Goodpaster and Nash, *Policies and Persons: A Casebook in Business Ethics* (New York: McGraw-Hill, Inc., 1991), p. 111.

limited to the business world? The academy practices its own version of an opaque paper-chase in, *e.g.*, the elevation of publishing—counted by the page and the refereed journal—over teaching—reckoned by the development of minds and spirits, which has produced its own distortions in higher education.

Solution: Integrating Just with Strategic Pay. The solution to this problem does not rest on selected programs, such as skill-based pay or gainsharing; it consists, rather, in a "way of thinking." The integration of the just wage tradition with strategic thinking will not occur through some sophisticated, programmatic technique, but through the way in which individual managers and firms think through the pay-relationship. Much, perhaps everything, will depend upon their willingness to entertain the profound human question, "Is the person made for work or is work, including technology, meant to serve the person?"[76] Certainly, the possibility of an integrated, just-and-strategic system of pay hangs upon it, and those who would honor the Judeo-Christian tradition must answer the question with an affirmation of the person over work, of virtue over technique. Such an affirmation, however, need not rest merely on the authority of a rich and venerable tradition. Person *over* work, and virtue *over* technique: these affirmations reflect a distinction between what is most *fundamental* and what is most *excellent* about a human organization.

What is most fundamental to an organization concerns its survivability. By enhancing profitability and efficiency, strategic pay strengthens a firm's chances for survival. Heinz's incentive plan was clearly driven by the judgment that consistent growth in earnings would guarantee survival of the company.

Yet, what is fundamental to an organization is not what is most excellent about it. Organizational survival is a means to the development of the person and community. While pay strategies focus on the survivability of the organization, they tend to ignore those questions concerning pay that go to the most excellent, human, dimensions of the firm: Does it pay justly? does it respect the subjective dimension of workers and their work, or is it concerned only with their productive capacities? does it foster authentic human development? Entrepreneurs and human resource managers must face the enormous challenge of integrating the economic and social development of the organization, marginalizing nei-

---

76. Pinckaers, *The Sources of Christian Ethics*, p. 87.

ther in favor of the other. In this connection, the Heinz incentive episode amounts to a cautionary tale: Heinz encouraged managers to become economic giants, at the expense of becoming moral dwarfs.

The integration of strategic with—let us call it—normative thinking is most critical for organizations in times of economic crisis, when wage-rates collide with falling revenues. Because, for many companies, compensation represents one of the highest costs of production, managing wages and bonuses is especially critical to the organization's economic order and sustainability when revenue decreases. Addressing this problem in a way that takes full advantage of strategic insight, while anchoring the solution in a framework of justice, can strengthen human relationships within the firm, even as it helps safeguard the firm's fiscal integrity.

When, for example, one of Reell Precision Manufacturing's largest customers, Apple Computer, cut back its orders, Reell's revenue fell significantly, threatening, if not the firm's survival, at least its size. Reell reacted in fully "strategic" fashion. Recognizing that its economic health was at stake, Reell addressed its shortfalls by reducing wages and salaries, and also by seeking a wider customer base through international markets, looking for greater efficiencies, reduced costs and new products, working to retain customers, *etc.* But Reell's response to this economic crisis proceeded in the context of, and was ordered by, what is at the heart of the firm as a human enterprise: the growth of people. As Reell reduced wages and salaries, executives took the larger cuts by percentage, and those employees under or at Reell's target wage were exempt from reductions.[77] Layoffs, which—for many companies—would have been the expedient of first resort, were seen at Reell as the last alternative, owing to the impact they could not fail to make on the relationships Reell had established as a work-community.

While Reell has, of course, found the experience of crisis painful, it has also found in it a catalyst of workplace solidarity. Organizational crises tend either to divide work communities or to unite them; no firm can expect to emerge from crisis unchanged.[78] If the leadership of a company

---

77. The strategic lesson is, of course, that if a company's system of compensation relies exclusively on fixed wages, during difficult times its room for maneuver will be severely limited. Moreover, the fixed wage tends to detach the perception of pay from pay's sources: productivity and revenue.

78. Moreover, when sacrifices are not distributed equitably throughout the workforce, organizations become downright dysfunctional. When, for example, General Motors demanded wage concessions from its unions, then awarded a round of executive bonuses, labor

can respond to a crisis justly and competently, by means which call for equitable sacrifice *from*—as opposed to sacrifice *of*—employees, sacrifice itself can prove to be a tonic for the work-community: it can result at once in a sounder economic organization (the fundamentals) and a more vital human community (excellence). Most employees are willing to undertake sacrifice when they believe it to be *shared* sacrifice which addresses a *common* threat.[79] In this connection, a preexisting culture of ownership (such, *e.g.*, as was promoted by Reell's employee stock plan) will go a long way toward eliciting willing sacrifice when business conditions make sacrifice unavoidable.

Reell, then, presents an example of a company which has learned to integrate normative and strategic thinking: it is a just organization which is strategically minded. Reell understands that human development, as its over-arching end, must be pursued through the virtues—foremost among them, justice; it employs strategic techniques in their proper place, as means of sustaining the company's human vocation.

4. Conclusion

Were a company committed to achieving a just wage tomorrow, what steps should its management take today? Three seem critically important:

(1) *Articulate a pay philosophy*. Every company adheres to an implicit philosophy of compensation; relatively few articulate it explicitly for themselves.[80] The three principles of a living wage (need), an equitable wage (contribution), and a sustainable wage (economic order) make for good starting-points. Of course, a philosophy of pay makes sense only for an organizational culture which finds its purpose in the common good of its members.

(2) *Evaluate present pay practices*. The three principles also make for critical standards against which to evaluate the present pay

---

was enraged by the display of executive egoism. Compared to Ford and Chrysler—whose management shared the pain of hard times—GM has subsequently suffered more frequent strikes, poorer morale, higher levels of employee distrust, and lower product quality.

79. Interestingly, Reell once instituted salary freezes in anticipation of a revenue shortfall which never materialized, generating some ill will among employees who thought the freeze unnecessary. Management learned to sacrifice in the event, not in anticipation of the event.

80. Lawler, *Strategic Pay*, p. 40.

system, with the aim of establishing a better fit between the norms of justice and concrete practice.

(3) *Align practice with philosophy*. Initiate policies that clearly respond to the principles of the just wage: *e.g.*, a "Living Wage Policy" which establishes a "floor" and connects employees' skill-development to wage-increases, or a "Wage Differential Policy" which confines wage-extremes within fixed ratios. Announced principles must receive concrete expression: an organization is usually better off with no principles than with principles that are not lived up to.[81]

These steps will not "solve" the "problem" of just pay. Rather, they will set an organization on a long, arduous and incremental path toward developing organizational conditions which foster both economic success and the moral and spiritual development of the work-community's members: owners, managers, employees.

---

81. *Ibid.*, p. 53.

A View from Management:
A Response to Michael Naughton

Richard Holmberg

Before I come to the substance of my remarks, I want, first, to thank Mr. Henning for the life he's lived; for the example he has given—and is —which brings us here today, and has prompted Mr. Naughton's presentation.

Second, having had the opportunity over the past week to spend some considerable time contemplating the themes of this conference, and having heard the papers presented thus far, I want to assure you all that what we are about here is far from merely "academic": it is absolutely topical; and I mean: for that famous "real world" of business.

That is, of course, the perspective I can bring to these discussions: the perspective of one who graduated from Saint Mary's College and went into business; who returned to Saint Mary's, after seventeen years of hands-on experience, for an MBA, looking to pick up specific skill-sets for business; and who spends his time now in management.

Let me say that, as a manager, I find Mr. Naughton's whole presentation to the point. But let me take up some of his thoughts which seem especially topical: first, those which treat the organization as a community of work. That concept seems to depend on communication among managers and their people, and I would suggest that management, right now, is in the throes of trying to address the difficult question of connecting meaningfully with our people. It is increasingly apparent to me as a manager that if I—and if *we*—as the management of our company, cannot connect with our people in a meaningful way; if we do not enable them—not only to *feel* like participants— but to actually participate in, and to contribute to, the shaping of our business, then I am— we are—not serving our company well, and delivering it a competitive disadvantage as well.

Professional management today really comes down to a core question, "How do I communicate in a way that is not 'hierarchical'—not demeaning, not diminishing—but which clearly recognizes who I am speaking with and, more importantly, what they can bring to the organization?" After all, people execute business plans; people interact; people communicate the values of the company; people either relegate management, relegate me, to a hollow, dinning bell at the top—speaking, but to no purpose—or people bring the value of what I say alive by taking it to purpose.

I'm trying to bring across that the core values of management are not so far from the kind of working relationships Mr. Naughton has described. Management begins in caring—about what really happens in the organization, and about the people who make it happen. And it depends on being able to communicate that you really do care, that you're willing to listen, that you're willing to empower people to understand their work more and do it better.

There's a philosophy making its way through business right now of more and more information for every worker. For example, we have a philosophy in our company that our books should be open. Financial information is for everyone: we want all our people to understand it, because the more people who understand it, the more they can impact it; the more they understand it, the more they will feel, not a "victim" of, but a participant in the success or the failure of the organization.

So, the principles Mr. Naughton has brought forward (and I very much look forward to talking with him more) on management as a kind of moral leadership, over and above "business skills," seem to me to be a part of a good management education, and they are in any case an important part of what we actually do as professional managers. You can go through your MBA program—learn statistics, write significant regressions, go through marketing and devise tremendous strategies—but if you cannot rally people, you're not really managing: you limit yourself competitively, and you risk doing the greatest injustice to everyone, which is to "lead" the organization to failure.

Second, increasing communication touches on the whole question of pay. We believe that information brings responsibility and accountability: if you're placed in a position to do more, you have a responsibility to use that position and to accept accountability for the use you make of it. And we believe that if you make people more responsible *and* more accountable, then you are in a better position to offer them a wage which meets their needs, and then some. So Mr. Naughton's thoughts on how skill-based and knowledge-based pay, and pay-for-performance, might contribute toward realizing the ideal of the just wage connects.

That said, I see great difficulties in practice. The subjective nature of compensation is probably one of the biggest challenges. The argument for the living wage makes sense, but we all—all managers—recognize the strategic limits to pay. We can't downplay the hard facts of sustain-abilty: the organization has to succeed financially if it is to continue as a vehicle whereby people can make a life.

Organizations like ours, for example, have branches around the United States. Some are prospering; some aren't. That doesn't mean that everyone isn't working hard—getting up, putting in as much effort as they can, having as much enthusiasm, possibly working with a better set of skills. But for some, the result just isn't there, and for others it is. That's the situation we face.

Now, performance-based pay happens to be an idea we've put a lot of thought into over some time. In the end, it seems to be very emotionally draining for people, especially with an adverse macro-economic situation that they can't control. And there's the opposite, people benefiting from a favorable economic situation they didn't make. Where does wage equity come in? So, the reality, it seems to me, is that skill and performance and the economic situation rarely play together in a way that would make skill-based or performance-based pay effective.

Still, I am convinced that the just wage is a concept that business needs to confront. That it's a Catholic concept needn't get in the way if we can put it forward to open-minded people not just as the right thing to do, but as something that makes business sense, and I think Mr. Naughton's approach is on the way there.

I really believe that the way to prosperity is for people to take responsibility for change at all levels, from the lowest to highest. I believe businesses have the responsibility and the opportunity to provide occasions where change can really take place, and that real change—real development—will not come out of large capital systems, but from individual companies based on one another and working with one another: individual businesses working, through management that works, in multicultural environments throughout the world. That's the environment in which individuals taking professional responsibility have the biggest impact. It should be possible to train managers, for that kind of environment, who see how they might go about achieving just wages, and how just wages might promote competitive advantages.

5

The Meaning of Solidarity

J. Michael Stebbins

I

Introduction

Since the Second Vatican Council, the concept of solidarity has assumed increasing prominence in Catholic social teaching and in Catholic social thought generally. It is a central theme of Pope John Paul II's writings and addresses on social issues. As he himself said when he stopped in Baltimore during his 1995 visit to the United States, "Since the beginning of my papal ministry, I have repeatedly affirmed the importance of social solidarity as an instrument for building up the civilization of love for which humanity yearns."[1] Church leaders often make explicit use of the concept of solidarity to diagnose social ills and to prescribe social remedies. Cardinal Roger Mahony of Los Angeles, for instance, publicly opposed Proposition 209, which aimed to dismantle state affirmative action programs in California, on the grounds that it would deal a serious

---

1. John Paul II, "Catholic Relief Services and Church Social Teaching," *Origins* 25, 18 (October 19, 1995), p. 315. Cf. also the many references to solidarity in the Index of *Dignity of Work: John Paul II Speaks to Managers and Workers*, ed. Gary Atkinson, Robert G. Kennedy, and Michael Naughton (Lanham, Maryland: University Press of America, 1994). In *Centesimus annus*, the Pope notes that what is meant by "solidarity" was a concern of Catholic social thought long before the term came into use: "What we nowadays call the principle of solidarity...is clearly seen to be one of the fundamental principles of the Christian view of social and political organization. This principle is frequently stated by Pope Leo XIII, who uses the term *friendship*, a concept already found in Greek philosophy. Pope Pius XI refers to it with the equally meaningful term *social charity*. Pope Paul VI, expanding the concept to cover the many modern aspects of the social question, speaks of a *civilization of love*" (*Centesimus annus* n. 10).

blow to the hard-won gains in interracial solidarity that had been made in that state.[2] Not surprisingly, solidarity now appears on everyone's short list of the fundamental principles of Catholic social teaching. In fact, some commentators maintain that it is the single term which best captures the basic orientation of that teaching.[3]

As people who want to communicate the message of Catholic social teaching effectively to a fragmented and disoriented world, we need to speak clearly about the meaning of solidarity. What is it? What is its source? How do we recognize it when it occurs? What can we do to promote and sustain it? I raise these questions because—as I listen to homilies, read articles in the Catholic press, and speak with workers in Catholic social ministries—I find that the term "solidarity" is often used without being carefully defined. Its very familiarity can have the effect of lulling us into a false sense of confidence that we already fully appreciate what it means.

In his 1987 encyclical, *Sollicitudo rei socialis*, John Paul discusses solidarity at some length. There, he characterizes it as an "attitude" or "virtue." It emphatically is "not a feeling of vague compassion or shallow distress at the misfortunes of so many people, both near and far"; rather, it is "a firm and persevering determination to commit oneself to the common good."[4] I propose to take this definition as a jumping-off point for exploring the notion of solidarity. In order to gain a rounded view of what solidarity is, we have to have some idea of what the common good is, some idea of what it means to commit oneself to the common good, and some idea of what it means to say that this commitment takes the form of a virtue. Those are the three topics I want to treat.

---

2. Cardinal Roger Mahony, "Affirmative Action and Catholic Social Teaching," *Origins* 25, 6 (June 22, 1995), pp. 89, 91-94. On the importance of solidarity in relation to the issue of debt reduction as a step toward promoting development in the Third World, cf. Cardinal Roger Etchegaray, "Golden Key of Solidarity," *The Tablet* (June 29, 1996), pp. 846-847.

3. Cf., *e.g.*, Monsignor Diarmuid Martin, "What the Church Tries to Do at International Conferences," *Origins* 25, 6 (June 22, 1995), pp. 94-98, and Archbishop Justin Rigali, "What Church Teaching Is: An Overview," *Origins* 26, 14 (September 19, 1996), pp. 216-219.

4. *Sollicitudo rei socialis*, n. 38.

II

The Common Good

For the classical philosophical tradition, the common good is the good of the whole community, considered precisely *as* a whole. Since a whole is composed of parts, the common good includes the good of the different parts of the community, whether groups or individuals—yet, it is the good of those parts considered, not in isolation, but in relation to all the other parts with which they form a functioning whole. Catholic social teaching shares this basic understanding of the common good, but also insists that, though individual persons are oriented to community and find their identity there, they are also ends in themselves. Consequently, it sees the common good as being realized to the extent that a community becomes the kind of place within which each of the persons who belong to it is able to achieve his or her proper fulfillment as a human being made in God's image.[5]

i. An Authentic Scale of Values

Fulfillment involves having one's needs and desires met—but not, of course, indiscriminately. We are a welter of competing needs and desires, and becoming a mature human being is largely a matter of sorting these out: of learning to distinguish between higher and lower needs, between authentic and inauthentic desires, and of discovering that we are at our best when we give ourselves over to the rhythms of what is highest and best in us. Hence, the common good is present to the extent that the goods produced in a given community are made available and are appropriated in a way that reflects what might be called humanly prioritized values.

In speaking about the issue of a scale of values, I am borrowing from the work of the Jesuit theologian, Bernard Lonergan.[6] His approach rep-

---

5. The common good "embraces the sum total of those conditions of social living, whereby men are enabled to achieve their own integral perfection more fully and more easily" (*Mater et magistra*, n. 65). Cf. also *Populorum progressio*, nn. 14-21, where this point is discussed in the context of a Christian perspective on human development. John Paul II uses Paul VI's notion of "complete humanism"—"the fully rounded development of the whole man and of all men"—as a way of defining the common good (*Sollicitudo rei socialis*, n. 38, quoting *Populorum progressio*, n. 42).

6. Cf. Bernard Lonergan, *Method in Theology*, 2nd ed. (Toronto: University of Toronto Press, 1973), Chapter 2.

resents an insightful way of presenting the position of Catholic social teaching on the objective hierarchy of goods. I am aware that what I am saying here is almost cryptic in its brevity, but I want at least to touch on the basic elements of this analysis in order to suggest its potential fruitfulness.

In general, a value is anything that meets a human want or need. This means that values are concrete, rather than abstract: they are actually existing goods of some kind, rather than principles. At one end of the scale are what might be called *vital* values, the values associated with biological life and health. They are the most basic human values, in that without them human life is cut off, so that there is no possibility of yet higher values emerging. *Social* values are higher than vital values: they are the roles, skills, institutions, and patterns of cooperation (a term about which I shall say more below) that make it possible to produce vital values more effectively, and to distribute them more widely. *Cultural* values are higher than social: they are the norms, symbols, stories and traditions that infuse social roles and institutions with meaning, and cause people to value one social order more than another (*e.g.*, democracy over monarchy). *Personal* values are realized whenever actual human beings and their communities live according to the standards of intelligence and responsibility. They are located at this point on the scale because vital, social and cultural values are not for their own sake, but are for the sake of making it possible for human persons and their communities to live authentically. Finally, and at the top of the scale, *religious* values are persons and communities who have been transformed by God's love. These represent the highest level of value because the personal value realized in authentic human living finds its ultimate fulfillment in persons' surrender to, and empowerment by, the all-embracing gift of God's love. This analysis implies that when a choice has to be made between or among goods, those that embody higher values should be chosen: they are better, more worthwhile and, hence, more choice-worthy than those that embody lower values.

What makes the lower values lower and the higher higher? It is the fact that higher values not only build on lower, but go beyond them. The truth of this statement can be seen most clearly, perhaps, by noting that the means for overcoming a deficiency of value on any lower level often lies at a higher level. For instance, if vital values such as adequate nutrition or vaccination against common diseases are to be made widely available within a community, then there is a need to think out and implement a social order capable of providing the requisite technology, education, economic arrangements, and political policies. But social institutions cannot remain just and effective unless they are infused with humanly authentic meanings—with what we have called cultural values. A family is not likely to remain intact for long, if the husband and wife do not recognize the permanence of their commitment as a value. Cultural values, in turn, cannot remain authentic, unless they are promoted and cherished by responsible persons. Here one can think of any number of people in public life who use the language of the American political heritage in a way that ends up undermining the meanings which that language was originally intended to convey. Finally, the possibility of steady growth in the ability to act responsibly depends crucially on the gift of God's love, the grace which opens our eyes to the values God sees in the world, and our hearts to love as God loves us.[7]

To talk about a scale of values is to invite a debate. We live in a culture in which there is no consensus about the meaning of human existence, and we find ourselves faced with serious disagreements about how values ought to be ordered, or whether they can be ordered at all. Sometimes a person who takes issue with the scale of values articulated in Catholic social teaching can be brought around by argument or dialogue. Sometimes, however, the disagreement stems less from contrary opinion than from disordered fears, antagonisms or desires that may be only dimly recognized; these are not responsive to any kind of human persuasion. In such cases, the impasse can be broken only by conversion—the heart of stone being plucked out and replaced by a heart of flesh—an event that is the work of God's grace (even if unrecognized as such by the person who experiences it). This realignment of desire results in "a new self looking out at the world,"[8] a self better attuned to the range of val-

---

7. Fred Lawrence describes the scale of values more succinctly: "At the core of any ethos...is a normative scale of values: *vital* values condition and are subordinate to *social* values such as a prosperous economy; social values condition and are subordinate to *cultural* values that give meaning and value to a society's way of life; these cultural values condition and serve *personal* values— the freedom and dignity of each human being; and all these values condition and are oriented and fulfilled by *religious* values relating us directly to divine transcendence" (from the Editor's Introduction to Bernard J. F. Lonergan, S. J., *An Essay in Circulation Analysis*, ed. Frederick G. Lawrence, Patrick H. Byrne, and Charles C. Helfing, to appear from the University of Toronto Press as a volume in *Collected Works of Bernard Lonergan*).

8. Joseph A. Komonchak, *Foundations in Ecclesiology* (supplementary issue of the *Lonergan Workshop* journal, v. 11), p. 47.

ues that shine forth in authentic human living. Whatever one makes of all this, there is no getting around the fact that Catholic social teaching claims that there is an objective scale of value like the one I have just outlined, and claims that it is a transcultural reality, a dynamic structure inherent in all authentic human desiring and choosing. The notion of the common good, then, goes hand-in-hand with the notion of an authentic scale of values.

ii. Patterns of Cooperation

Now I want to turn to another crucial aspect of the common good, namely, the fact that it involves patterns of cooperation. The common good is not to be found in some single instance of a particular human need being met; rather, it is to be found in a cooperative setup that succeeds in meeting the needs of many people on an ongoing basis. These patterns may be formal or informal, obvious or obscure, efficient or inefficient, the result of careful planning or of mere happenstance.

An illustration of what I mean by "patterns of cooperation" can be had by considering the green beans that I cajoled my three-year-old daughter into eating the other night. How did they end up on her plate? As it turns out, her need for nutrition—and, derivatively, my need to feel like I was being a responsible parent—were met by a host of interacting people and routines: the employees of the grocery store in their interrelated functions; the corporation that owns the store; the suppliers of the products sold by the store, and the bank that handles its money; the outfits that maintain its cooling and heating equipment; the trucking company, or companies, that transported the beans; the manufacturer of the truck, and the people associated with its maintenance; the builders, planners, financiers and maintainers of the roads the truck uses; the grower of the beans and the laborers who picked them...and the seed company, the fertilizer producer, the chemical company that produced the pesticides used on the bean crop...Companies that specialize in advertising played their role throughout the process. Government was involved at many junctures by way of laws, regulations and policies regarding food quality, taxation, interstate commerce, employment, public health, land and water management and so on. The communication that had to take place to make all this interaction possible required still further layers of activity and participation, as did everything involved in my being able to go to the grocery store, to purchase the beans, and to cook and serve them.

The example is complex, but the point is fairly simple. In contemporary society, the common good is the product of human cooperation on a grand scale. It incorporates vast numbers of people; its structure is constituted by an intricate web of organizations, institutions, and routinized processes and transactions; it calls for highly developed differentiation of roles and specialization of skills. Yet, despite the high degree of coordination it involves, for the most part this cooperative activity occurs without the guiding hand of a centralized authority. It should also be pointed out that in our contemporary situation of increasing global interdependence, it becomes practically impossible to talk about the common good of any group without reference to the common good of the world community.

What this analysis underscores is the crucial part human intelligence plays in the emergence and maintenance of the common good. It requires intelligence to come up with new particular goods—an enhanced microprocessor, say, or a poem that grips the imagination. It requires intelligence to devise patterns of cooperation, or to keep them functioning when conditions change—think of the many challenges facing entrepreneurs or managers in setting up or running a business. Moreover, it requires the intelligence of many people, each trying to understand the sphere within which he or she operates, each communicating what he or she has found out, and each learning from what others have found out. This collaborative ingenuity and self-correcting process of learning is a *sine qua non* of the common good.

Working for the common good, then, implies a concern not just for producing humanly valuable goods, but also for intelligently devising, operating within, maintaining, coordinating and improving patterns of cooperation capable of producing such goods effectively.

iii. How do we get there from here?

The common good is a dynamic, rather than a static, reality. This is true in two respects. First, we are always "on the way" to the common good, because it is never fully realized in any community or society. Second, the fact that communities change over time means that the concrete realization of the common good, however partial and fragmentary it may be, has to change as well.

The second point requires a bit of elaboration. Although the basic hierarchy of values remains constant over time and across cultures, the particular needs of particular people in particular communities will vary; as they vary, so will the arrays of goods provided to meet them, and so will the patterns of cooperation needed to produce the goods. Nutrition has always been a human value, but no one in imperial Rome would have known what to do with a microwave oven. Health has always been a human value, but no one in the 1960s had been identified as needing an AIDS vaccine. Patterns of cooperation, and the goods produced by them, have to develop and shift constantly to keep up with new needs or to meet old needs more efficiently. This means that a key aspect of the intelligence required to promote the common good is the ability to grasp the concrete potentialities, latent in each situation, that could give rise to new and better goods, new and better patterns of cooperation. Attentiveness, imagination, and the appreciation of complexity are all required.

Again, the fact of development does not mean that the common good ever develops along a smooth, uninterrupted line of pure progress. There are plenty of failed experiments along the way. Institutions can outlive their usefulness. Opportunities for new goods and for new cooperative structures can remain unexploited, because people lack the financial resource or the political muscle to make them actual. The unconverted can place insurmountable obstacles in the path of what would be reasonable solutions to problems. The ideas needed to meet a particular set of needs may simply be lacking. In any event, the common good is always only partially realized. It is a work-in-progress, not a finished product. To the extent that it actually exists in any community, it is always intertwined with other elements of the social situation whose origins can be traced to sin, ignorance, stupidity, ill will or plain bad luck.

III

Commitment to the Common Good

Just to recall where my remarks have been and where they are headed: I am trying to explicate the meaning of John Paul II's claim that solidarity is a virtue consisting in "a firm and persevering determination to commit oneself to the common good." Up to this point, I have been highlighting certain aspects of the common good, which can be summarized as follows: the common good is the product of properly oriented human freedom and collaborative human intelligence; a community achieves its common good to the extent that its patterns of cooperation, and the particular goods flowing from them, concretely embody an authentic hierarchy of value. If this is, in fact, an accurate—albeit an admittedly sketchy—depiction of the common good, then what does it mean for us to commit ourselves to the common good? To put the question another way, what kind of actions give expression to the virtue of solidarity?

As John Paul II has put it, the exercise of solidarity is "the love and service of neighbor, especially of the poorest."[9] In this sense, every kind of action that reaches out in love to meet the real needs of people is a manifestation of solidarity. The greater the need—and this is the point of the preferential option for the poor—the more insistent is the call to love and service. Furthermore, what solidarity demands is not so much working *for* others as working *with* them— hence John Paul's statement that the act proper to solidarity is collaboration.[10] And the source of this activity, the motive that impels us to take on others' burdens as our own and to join with with them in the effort to promote their own integral development, is not some theory or ideology. Rather, it is a real apprehension of the fact of human interdependence.[11] That apprehension may emerge as a gradually dawning awareness, or it may erupt as an unsettling disruption of our usual way of looking at ourselves and the world—that reorientation that might best be described as religious or moral conversion.[12] Whatever the path by which we arrive at that insight, its emotional component is undeniable: it includes a felt sense of identification with all human beings, and especially with those whose concrete needs are most familiar. I do not at all want to downplay this affective aspect of solidarity. If our commitment to social action does not spring from a spontaneous consciousness of oneness and mutuality with those whom we serve, then the acts we are engaging in, however praiseworthy they may be in themselves, are expressions of something other than solidarity.

---

9. *Sollicitudo rei socialis*, n. 46.

10. *Ibid.*, n. 39 (emphasis in original). Cf. also Donald Dorr, *Option for the Poor: A Hundred Years of Catholic Social Teaching*, rev. ed. (Maryknoll, New York: Orbis Books, 1992, pp. 3-6, 234.

11. *Sollicitudo rei socialis*, n. 38.

12. John Paul II speaks of "the urgent need to change the spiritual attitudes which define each individual's relationship with self, with neighbor, with even the remotest human communities, and with nature itself" (*loc. cit.*).

Having said this, however, I would go on to claim that Catholic social teaching's clear articulation of a link between solidarity and the common good challenges us to conceive of solidarity as showing itself especially in a concern for designing and maintaining patterns of cooperation. Giving a hungry person a meal is an exercise of solidarity. Setting up a soup kitchen and keeping it running month after month is a greater exercise of solidarity. Addressing the systemic economic, psychological, political, social and cultural issues that put people in the position of needing soup kitchens, represents an even greater exercise of solidarity.

Every concrete manifestation of solidarity is a good and worthy thing. The point I am trying to make, though, is that taking solidarity seriously means taking upon ourselves, with respect to particular situations, the responsibility of understanding accurately the patterns of cooperation that are already in place, with all their desirable and undesirable consequences; taking solidarity seriously means accepting responsibility for seeing where real development could take place, and where it would be folly to attempt development, at least for the moment; it means taking responsibility for carefully thinking out the many practical steps that would have to be taken in order to bring a new and better situation out of the old. The new world which solidarity calls us to build is a labor not only of love, but of creative and collaborative intelligence. Most of us will do our work for the common good on a relatively small scale—in our families, in a university department, in a parish, in a business. Still, the kind of difference we are able to make in those settings will depend in large part on the degree to which we successfully deal with the cooperative patterns that structure what goes on there.[13]

I stress the significance of patterns of cooperation for two reasons. The first is that it is relatively easy for Christians committed to social justice to utter prophetic denunciations of this or that institution, organizational practice, or social situation. While in many cases such denunciations may be entirely appropriate, there is a danger of assuming that our duty to act in solidarity has been fulfilled once we have pointed out what is wrong.

---

13. I am struck by the suggestion of Michael J. Naughton and Thomas Bausch, in "The Integrity of a Catholic Management Education" (*California Management Review* 34, 8 (Summer, 1996), pp. 12-13), that management students at Catholic schools ought to be encouraged to offer their managerial skills to help do strategic planning for small, hard-pressed businesses in economically disadvantaged neighborhoods. This amounts to setting up a pattern of cooperation (the service program run by the university) aimed at helping people set up patterns of cooperation (successfully functioning businesses).

The far more difficult job, it seems to me, is to engage in the process of figuring out concretely what ought to come next and how we might make it happen.

The second reason for emphasizing the importance of patterns of co-operation is to draw attention to the huge amount of intellectual work that must accompany our efforts to promote the common good. John Paul is correct when he says that the social message of the Church "will gain credibility more immediately from the witness of actions than as a result of its internal logic and consistency."[14] By the same token, social actions based on inadequate theory are apt to do more harm than good in the long run. At this point in history, the social sciences are still, at best, only in their adolescence. We lack the tools to understand all the dynamisms of human living that are relevant to anticipating what the common good of a particular community would be and to implementing its emergence. Economists, for example, frankly admit that they do not understand the business cycle.[15] Until they do, we really will not know how to anticipate and smooth out the downturns that wreak so much economic havoc when they occur. We do not really understand how to reform the welfare system, how to fix the schools, how to combat the drug problem effectively, and so on. The question in these connections does not involve merely an absence of political will, but involves real deficiencies in data-gathering, theorizing and testing, in the range of questions being asked, and in the creativity and sophistication of the solutions being proposed. Living responsibly at the level of our times demands in turn a collaborative intellectual enterprise that will not shrink from confronting the world in all its concrete complexity.[16]

In sum, the commitment to solidarity implicates the head as much as it does the heart. If our desires are skewed, then we will not act at all; and if our thinking is inept, the results of our actions will likely run counter

---

14. *Centesimus annus*, n. 57.

15. Cf. Paul Krugman, *Peddling Prosperity: Economic Sense and Nonsense in the Age of Diminished Expectations* (New York: W.W. Norton & Co., 1994), p. 24.

16. John Paul acknowledges the need for interdisciplinary study: "[T]he Church's social teaching has an important interdisciplinary dimension. In order better to incarnate the one truth about man in different and constantly changing social, economic, and political contexts, this teaching enters into dialogue with the various disciplines concerned with man. It assimilates what these disciplines have to contribute, and helps them to open themselves to a broader horizon, aimed at serving the individual person, who is acknowledged and loved in the fullness of his or her vocation" (*Centesimus annus*, n. 59).

to our intentions. Living in solidarity requires the full and integrated engagement of *all* our specifically human capacities.

IV

Solidarity as a Virtue

I will conclude with a few brief remarks about the significance of characterizing solidarity as a virtue. The issue here is a personal one. What kind of people do we have to be to commit ourselves to the extraordinarily difficult task of promoting the common good? How do we sustain our intellectual and moral—which is to say, practical—efforts? Clearly, having what John Paul calls "a feeling of vague compassion or shallow distress" is not going to do the job. What is needed is something far deeper and more abiding, a spring for *sustained* action. This is what the Pope is driving at when he calls solidarity a virtue. For, a virtue is a habit, a developed capacity to perform a certain kind of activity easily, excellently and with enjoyment. The virtue of solidarity in this sense is a deeply rooted orientation of our entire selves. To the extent that we possess it, we are people whose minds and hearts turn spontaneously to the task of serving the common good, even in the face of opposition and difficulty.

Like most habits, the virtue of solidarity has to be acquired gradually. It requires a lengthy process of educating one's feelings and sensibilities, of acquiring knowledge, of broadening and deepening one's experience of the lives of other people, of finding opportunities for engaging in service, and so on. How do we help people enter into this process in a truly effective way? Speaking only about efforts being undertaken by the Catholic Church, are our current preaching and teaching about faith and justice, our liturgies, our service programs in schools and parishes, addressing this need adequately? Would the problem be solved if we simply did more of what we are already doing? I only raise the question here, but I suspect that, despite the good that is already being done, a serious and concerted effort to inculcate the virtue of solidarity would take us far beyond current efforts.

Finally, what makes it possible, ultimately, for us to live a life marked by solidarity in the serious sense is the experience of God's limitless love for us, the love which, St. Paul says, "has been poured out in our hearts through the Holy Spirit who has been given to us" (Romans 5:5). Only that love can give us the assurance, the peace and the single-hearted commitment to overcome the obstacles — internal and external — that hinder us from living with a sustained spirit of love for the good of all, even of those who wish to be our enemies. In the end, any success we achieve in attaining the common good is more God's doing than ours. Solidarity is not our own "project." It is, rather, our cooperation in the divine plan, our participation in the creating and redeeming presence of God in the world.

Solidarity and Mystery:
A Response to J. Michael Stebbins

Dan Cawthon

I want to thank Michael Stebbins for his very illuminating analysis of the concept of solidarity. His presentation is helpful for distinguishing solidarity from what Pope John Paul calls a "feeling of vague compassion" or "shallow distress at the misfortunes of so many people."

Dr. Stebbins touches upon a dichotomy which, it seems to me, solidarity yokes together—the one and the many, the individual and the collective. The name "Adam," as you know, means not only "this one man," but also "the human race." "Male and female," the Scripture has it, "God created *Adam*"; that is, God created Adam as both "self" and "other." Paradoxically, then, to develop oneself as an individual involves a commitment to the common good. *The* problem of life, it seems to me, is to put those two together in some way. The examination of the concept of solidarity has provided fruitful suggestions for achieving this synthesis.

Solidarity runs counter to the popular notion that my identity is attained by fulfilling *my* needs and *my* desires (or, to use the jargon of the day, "I've got to be me, got to find out who I am and then go out and accomplish it!"), implying that I am compelled by God and the culture around me to fulfill my need, with no concern for others.

Solidarity implies that the compulsion to "fulfill myself" leads me, rather, to turn towards the "other"—*i.e.*, to fulfill a need outside myself. In other words, as I respond to the need of someone outside myself, I am —by that action—fulfilling my need to achieve self-identity. Solidarity points to this mystery.

Dr. Stebbins mentions that solidarity includes a felt sense of identification with all human beings. From this perspective, self-knowledge— self-identity—is always achieved indirectly, as I experience myself responding to the vital need of another human being. Thus self-knowledge is a reflective knowledge.

"Identity" is one of those words which, like "Adam," implies a dichotomy. On the one hand, it can point to the "uniqueness" of a person: to know my identity is to know myself as different from all others. On the other hand, it is related to the word "identical," suggesting sameness.

In the latter case, I find my *uniqueness* as I discover my *sameness* with others. The notion of solidarity unites that which, in our fallen state, seems contradictory.

I was also struck by the emphasis on the "ordering of desire," the argument that the deepest desire of each human being, the one which orders all others, is the desire to become one with that which is outside the self. The notion of solidarity leads to the awareness that the deepest need of the individual is to perceive and attend to the needs of those who are other. *Your* need and *my* need to discover who I am meet in the experience of solidarity.

This latter is the paradox which is described in the Gospels: "I was hungry, and you gave me to eat; I was thirsty, and you gave me to drink." The response, "When did I feed you, when did I give you to drink?" points to the fact that self-identity is achieved reflectively — it arrives through the back door. Similarly, the Gospels point out that to find one's life is to lose it, to lose it — on behalf of others — is to find it.

Another, very fruitful notion which the essay discusses is the need for the individual to identify with the needs of the *poor*. Last week, Father Elwood Kaiser was on campus at Saint Mary's to promote his new film, *Entertaining Angels*, which is about the life of Dorothy Day. One of the scenes in the film underscores, in a very moving way, the point Dr. Stebbins makes in his paper. When asked why she devotes herself to the poor, Day says: "Unless I do that, I have no access to the kingdom of God." Thus, solidarity implies not only that there is an intimate link between the need of the individual and the needs of others, but that, as the two are joined, we gain entrance into the kingdom of God.

In the last part of the essay, serving the patterns of cooperation within a culture is highlighted as another means of being in solidarity. There are, of course, problems with this notion. There are situations when such service seems the reverse of solidarity: we've heard of the priest, for example, who is so busy serving the ecclesiastical structure that he fails to attend to his flock, or of the politician who expends all of his energies in Washington, ignoring his constituency at home. So, while I agree that serving the structures of community is a way of achieving solidarity, I can see how problems arise — must arise? — in practice.

Contributors and Respondents

Thomas A. Cavanaugh, Assistant Professor of Philosophy, University of San Francisco, is an ethicist. His articles have appeared in such journals as *The Thomist, Aquinas Review, Philosophical Papers, Bioethics, Journal of Christian Bioethics*, and the *Cambridge Quarterly of Healthcare Ethics*.

Daniel Cawthon, Professor of Drama, Saint Mary's College of California, is known, among many other roles, for his stage portrayals of Fr. Damien of Molokai.

S. A. Cortright, Associate Professor of Philosophy, Saint Mary's College of California, is Director of the John F. Henning Institute.

Patrick Downey is Assistant Professor of Philosophy, Saint Mary's College of California, where he devotes himself to the teaching and study of ethics.

Edwin M. Epstein, Dean and Earl W. Smith Professor, School of Economics and Business Administration, Saint Mary's College of California, originated the Corporate Social Policy Process model, to aid analysis of corporate governance in the interests of social responsibility.

James Gordley, Shannon Cecil Turner Professor of Law, University of California, Berkeley, is the author, among numerous other works, of *The Philosophical Origins of Modern Contract Doctrine* (Oxford, 1991).

Wayne H. Harter, Assistant Professor of Philosophy, Saint Mary's College of California, is the author of the forthcoming *The Privileged Task*, a study of integrally Catholic education.

Richard Holmberg is President and Chief Executive Officer of John A. Wagner & Associates, one of San Francisco's largest privately held corporations, which supplies diversified building and consumer products, and conducts extensive international operations.

James B. Murphy, Associate Professor of Government, Dartmouth College, is the author, among other works, of *The Moral Economy of Labor: Aristotelian Themes in Economic Theory* (Yale University Press, 1993).

Michael J. Naughton, Associate Professor of Theology and Business, University of St. Thomas (St. Paul), and Director, Institute for Christian Social Thought and Management, is the author of *The Good Stewards: Practical Applications of the Social Vision of Work.*

Ernest S. Pierucci is a San Francisco business attorney and a member of the Board of Visitors of the Catholic University of America Columbus School of Law whose articles on integrating Catholic social thought with liberal and business education have appeared in such journals as *Issues in Catholic Higher Education* and the *Review of Business.*

J. Michael Stebbins, Senior Fellow, Woodstock Theological Center, Georgetown University, is the author of *The Divine Initiative: Grace, World-Order and Human Freedom in the Early Writings of Bernard Lonergan* (University of Toronto Press, 1995).

Indices

Select Index of Names

References to footnotes are given in **bold** type following the page number.

Index of Sources

References to footnotes are given in **bold** type following the page number.

Index of Select Topics

References to footnotes are given in **bold** type following the page number.

justice on property in another's possession (St. Thomas), 63, 71-72, 74-76; unmet need as the basis of the justificatory problem of full, "liberal" property-rights, 65-66; goods of the earth ordained by the Creator for the satisfaction of human need generally (common use doctrine of property), 11, 63, 69-72, 74-75, 81-82, 92 **19**; principle of need at the basis of the doctrine of the living wage, 92-94.

NEIGHBOR: exercise of solidarity defined as "love and service of neighbor" (John Paul II), 127.

ORGANIZATION (see also BUSINESS, EMPLOYER, FIRM): economic or objective dimensions (productivity, profit) of the organization as the focus of strategic theory, 87-88; exclusive focus on the organization's subjective dimensions a prelude to economic crisis, on its objective dimensions an invitation to moral stagnation, 89; systems of compensation as a condition for developing the right relations between employees and the organization, 89-91; distribution of training, developmental opportunities in U. S. organizations, 95-97; effectiveness of the organization enhanced by skill-based systems of compensation, 98-99; bearing of living wages on strategic anaylsis of the organization, 100-101; equitable wage relative to employee contributions to organizational success, 102; culture of the organization and gainsharing, 106-109; tension between fundamentals and excellence of the organization, 109-111, 112-113, illustrated (Reell Precision Manufacturing Co.), 113-114.

OWNERSHIP (see also PROPERTY): private ownership as a means to

common use of property, 11, 71-72; distinction between ownership (private possession) and use of property, 67-72, 74-76; ownership and community, 83; employee ownership as a means to organizational effectiveness, 107-108.

PAY (see also COMPENSATION, WAGE): incommensurable with the value of work, 35, 89; pay historically a token of just relations between employers and employees, 86-87; human resource management and strategic theories of pay, 87-88; tension between strategic and normative understandings of pay, 88-90; strategic understanding of pay necessary, but insufficient, for achieving just systems of pay, 91; **knowledge-based/skill-based pay**, 97-100: as a strategy for achieving living wages, 97-98; as a mode of enhancing the subjective rewards of work, 98-99; objections to knowledge/skill-based pay, 100-101; **pay equity**: principle of contribution, 102-103; **pay-for-performance**, 105-109: strategic categories of, 105 58; employees' acceptance of, 105 59, 106; direct linkage of pay to individual/team performance (gainsharing), 106-109; **sustainable pay**, 109-114: and principle of economic order, 109; strategic view of pay and normative principles, 109-112; integration of normative with strategic thinking on pay, 112-114.

PERSON: divided between intrinsically and instrumentally valuable pursuits, 4-5; as an "atom" of will, 5-6; and the nature of work (John Paul II), 13-15; the person's self-realization through work (Hegel, Marx), 26; "personalist argument" (John Paul II,